A Checkered Past

My 20 Years as Indy 500 Chief Steward

Tom Binford
with Florrie Binford Kichler

Cornerstone Press, Inc.
Carmel, Indiana

All photos courtesy of the Indianapolis Motor Speedway
Corporation.
All terms such as "Indy 500", "Indianapolis 500", "Indianapolis
500 Mile Race", and "500" are trademarks of the Indianapolis
Motor Speedway Corporation.

Cover art by Ron Burton, Speedway, Indiana

Cornerstone Press, Inc.
P. O. Box 1283
Carmel, Indiana 46032
317-844-6070

Publisher's Cataloging in Publication
(Prepared by Quality Books Inc.)

Binford, Thomas W., 1924-
    A checkered past : my 20 years as Indy 500 chief steward / by
Tom Binford with Florrie Binford Kichler.
    p. cm.
    Preassigned LCCN: 93-090170.
    ISBN 1-882859-01-4.

    1. Binford, Thomas W., 1924- 2. Indianapolis Speedway Race--
Officials and employees--Biography. 3. Automobile racing--
Officiating. I. Kichler, Florrie Binford. II. Title.

GV1033.5.I53B55 1993   796.72'068'77252'092
                                                                QBI93-575

10 9 8 7 6 5 4 3 2 1

Printed in the United States of America

To my husband, Mark, whose love
and support never wavers;
To our children, Brian and Sara, who kept
their heads while Mom was losing hers.

Florrie Binford Kichler

Table of Contents

Introduction

by Tony George

Tom Binford has been around the Indianapolis Motor Speedway longer than I have, and I've been around it all my life.

But the contents of this book aren't aimed at going back all those years to 1955 when Tom became a director of the United States Auto Club shortly after my grandfather chartered the organization. Nor does it go back to 1957 when he was elected president of USAC, a post he ably administered for 13 years. It doesn't even go back to when I was born, in 1959.

What lies ahead is the 20-year chronicle of Tom's reign as Chief Steward of the Indianapolis 500, a post he accepted after the incredibly difficult 1973 500 in what was a particularly dire historical moment for the Speedway.

My perception at the time—I was 13—was little more than awareness of the simple fact that Tom Binford had been entrusted with execution of my family's pride and joy, the "500."

Through the ensuing years, it was obvious to me, even though as I was growing up it struck me only in a passive way, that Tom had the competitive aspects of the "500" well in hand. And I remember that it seemed Tom was always moving from one prestigious post to another within the community. He was either running a bank, chairing a committee, collecting an award or being named president or director of assorted businesses and organizations. But I didn't spend a lot of time *noticing* what Tom was doing.

And then came late 1989 when I assumed the presidency of the facility that hosts the largest one-day sporting event in the world. It was then that I learned the intimidating aspects of real responsibility, and developed a deep appreciation for what Tom Binford has meant to the last 20 Indianapolis 500's.

Qualities that perhaps I had taken for granted in Tom quickly began to stand out. His ability to form a consensus among diverse opinions was amazing. His judgement and leadership were sure and firm. Decisions he makes reflect a wisdom and understanding forged through years of experience in all levels of racing and an incredible array of non-racing successes.

Consider the times of his stewardship. My grandfather, Tony Hulman, who had bought the Speedway in 1945 and led its operations for 32 years, died in 1977. The race car owners formed Championship Auto Race Teams (CART), and split away from USAC to run their own series with their own rules as the entire fabric of the business of auto racing changed. The technical aspects and costs of our racing lurched wildly forward.

And yet the 500 thrived. The traditions that sustain this event cannot be ignored and provided a powerful force in the survival of "The Greatest Spectacle in Racing." But in times as perilous as these past 20 years have been, the competition on the race track remained world-class.

I didn't even realize until late 1989 that the abiding, steady hand keeping this essence of the "500" safe was Tom Binford. Nor did I realize, until researching some information for this Introduction, that Tom provided this service to the Speedway while serving as director or president of enough business and civic organizations to fill a ten-page, single-spaced resume.

There is a story about a gathering in 1969 when Tom announced he was stepping down from his 13-year tenure as USAC president. I've been told my grandfather stood up, alone, and in a quiet voice that hushed an already nearly-silent crowd, said simply and spontaneously, "Tom, I don't know how anybody could have done the things you have done for USAC and racing."

I'll take this opportunity to echo those sentiments—nearly 25 years later—on behalf of my family and all the race competitors and fans who owe so much to Tom's efforts, his dignity and to the respect he has commanded over the years.

I'm looking forward to reading Tom's insights and commentary on these past 20 remarkable years at the Speedway, because nobody else has been as close to the action during this era as Tom has.

I'll only ask that these aren't his final racing memoirs.

Foreword

by Johnny Rutherford

During May, 1974, I remember some significant events occurring that had either an impact on my own career or on the Indianapolis 500 Mile Race. On the personal side, of course, was the fact that for the first time in eleven years, I finished the Race and won my first "Indy 500". Another fact was that Tom Binford was appointed to serve for the first time as Chief Steward of the famed Race.

To refresh your memory, that was also the year of the "energy crunch" which was felt by all across our nation. In an effort to respond to the plea to save fuel, the Indianapolis Motor Speedway and the United States Auto Club called for one week less of practice for the race teams, asked that four days of qualifying be consolidated into two days, and set reductions in fuel allotments.

Tom Binford, as Chief Steward, was charged with the responsibility of being the final authority in interpreting and applying the rules and procedures of the Race, pronouncing penalties resulting from rules violations and, most importantly, conducting the Race in the safest manner possible for all concerned. The 500 Mile Race encompasses all activities on the track from the time the track opens for practice until the Race is officially concluded.

Now, I want to tell you, Tom did not take these responsibilities lightly. As I was to find out, Tom had read the rules and was ready to interpret and enforce them as he felt they should be. Everyone, including my crew and me, thought that essentially nothing would change from years past. A miscalculation on our part!

During practice, I had been one of the fastest on the track, and had a more than good shot at the pole position on the first day of qualifying. As happens more than not at the track, my team suffered a minor crisis the morning of qualifying when I lost an engine in practice.

An engine change was completed in record time in the garage area. Qualifying began promptly at 11 am. The car was returned to the qualifying line after the 11 am start, but before my turn came to attempt qualification. When the crew tried to place the car in the position I had drawn for qualifying, officials informed them that, because the car was not in position when qualifying began, we would have to go to the end of the line.

In essence, this had the effect of moving us back to the third period of qualifications from the first! Sound confusing? You bet, and my chance for the coveted pole position would be lost.

I was not about to give up without a fight, and I had some support from one Al Unser, Sr. who had suffered the same fate I had. Together, we set out to find our new Chief Steward to inform him of his wrong call in the "new" interpretation of the rules.

Tom must have had a tough time keeping his cool. Al and I left no stone unturned as we explained in very "plain" language, accompanied by hand gestures, how we felt about his call. But keep his cool he did, and his ruling remained unchanged. With the second fastest qualifying time, I started the Race next to Al in the ninth row.

Fortunately, I weathered that storm to go on and win the Race in 1974; and fortunately for the drivers at the Indianapolis Motor Speedway, Tom Binford weathered the storm to remain as Chief Steward for the past 20 years.

Tom has remained consistent and has gained the respect of the racers for being fair and making the calls on rules enforcement in the best interest of all. Officials could never hope to win a popularity contest, as theirs is often a job conflicting with others who have a great deal at stake. Everything tends to happen quickly in racing, and officiating must keep pace by making calls rapidly with efficiency, effectiveness, and no bias. There are no instant replays here.

Most importantly, Tom Binford has had a very stabilizing effect during his tenure as Chief Steward. Speeds have escalated nearly 40 mph in the past 20 years, and rules for safety have been such a priority that the cars and the track operate in the safest atmosphere ever. The pressures under which the officials must operate have increased to new levels, and Tom has met the challenge.

Except for that one call in 1974, Tom Binford has almost always been right. Tom, my helmet is off to you!

Preface

by Tom Binford

A few months ago, my daughter, Florrie Kichler, called and in the course of the conversation suggested that I should write a book about my 20 years as Chief Steward of the Indianapolis 500. I backed off by saying that I didn't have time. "Why don't you take some of my weekly columns in the *Indianapolis Business Journal* and make a book out of them?"

She didn't accept my suggestion, at least for right now, and replied that time was no excuse. She'd do all the work and, by golly, she did— the research, the organizing and the first draft. All I had to do was make about twenty hours of tapes and do the rewrite, and I had a ball doing it.

I recommend it to all of you who have brilliant daughters in the publishing business. The best part will be the hours of time spent with your daughter. It's a rare opportunity.

I'm also blessed with a son, Bill Binford, whose vocation is engineering and avocation is auto racing. He read this manuscript for technical errors. Bill is a track officials at Indianapolis also, and is a great deal more experienced today than I was in 1974. Yes, Indy Car racing is a family sport. Just ask the Unsers, Andrettis, Carter/Parsons, Bettenhausens, Vukovich's, and Binfords.

"Great," you might be saying, "but why would anyone want to read a book about your life and, more to the point, why would anyone want to read about your 20 years as Chief Steward?" It's a good question. I'm not sure anyone would, but I have one thing going for me—the Indianapolis 500 Mile Race. It occupies a unique attraction in the world of auto racing...indeed in the world of sports. Known internationally as the oldest (since 1911), largest (over 300,000 spectators and a multi-million dollar purse), and most prestigious auto race in the world, it has a magnetic pull on participants and fans alike.

As far as I know, nobody has written a book about officiating at an auto race. And probably for good reason. However, this book does not attempt to be a "how-to-do-it" manual. It's more of a memoir regarding a 20-year period of the 500 related from a different viewpoint—that of an official.

If you are a fan of the 500, you might find it entertaining as well as revealing. If you're not, you might still find it intriguing. I hope so.

For those of you who don't know, the job of a Chief Steward is similar to the job of a Chief Executive Officer in a corporation. The Chief Steward of an auto race is literally personally responsible for the conduct of all racing activities, the application of the regulations and the determination of the finishing positions. The truth of the matter is practically all of the responsibilities are delegated to others. A Chief Steward is only as good as his team, and may be worse.

I have been fortunate to have a first-rate team of officials, some of whom have been with me for the full 20 years. Only one, however, has served as a steward and executive official for the entire period.

That is my strong right arm, Art Meyers, from the

Phoenix area. The current executive officials in addition to Meyers, who do so much so well and keep me out of trouble through their diligence and skills are, in order of years of service; Keith Ward, Steward and former Chief Observer; Bob Cassaday, Steward and Chief Observer; Rich Coy, Steward and Director of Certification; Mike Devan, Technical Director; Claude Fisher, Chief Observer; Art Graham, Director of Timing and Scoring; Les Kimbrell, Director of Scoring Operations; Jack Gilmore, Director of Safety; and Duane Sweeney, Chief Starter. Past heroes such as the late Frankie Delroy and Jack Beckley, former Technical Directors, and the late Lefty Hurt, former Chief Observer, should be credited as well as many others. There are actually close to 300 officials working in some capacity during the month of May.

I have also been blessed by the support and counsel of both Dick King, President of USAC, and Roger McCluskey, renowned race driver and USAC Executive Vice President. They are not officials at the track, but they help in many ways.

Lastly, I have been aided immeasurably by the solid support I have received from the Indianapolis Motor Speedway, especially Tony Hulman, who accepted me wholeheartedly before I had my rookie stripes off. Joe Cloutier and John Cooper gave me all the support I needed, and Tony George, current President and grandson of Tony Hulman, has continued the support. These four men shared one major character trait in the manner in which they carried out their duties. The pattern was set by Tony Hulman, and the character trait was humility.

They played and play the role of CEO of the Indianapolis Motor Speedway with humility, sensitivity and deference to the many loyal colleagues (many of whom are volunteers) who come together to perform the annual miracle of the 500 Mile Race.

Tony Hulman never referred to the IMS as "my track." He always treated it as if he were trustee of a national treasure. Tony didn't like to make decisions—he preferred to agree to a recommendation. He was a died-in-the-wool race fan, and the one thing that could get him riled enough to give an order was what he considered to be mistreatment of a fan. The crowds still reign between the pits and Gasoline Alley because Tony insisted the fans have continuous access to that area.

Tony was beloved by everyone...surely one of the most popular people in the state and deservedly so. His acts of kindness were legion. His highly competent and loyal assistant, June Swango, told me one of her most difficult jobs was trying to take care of all the people Tony made promises to during the course of the year...from gasoline attendants to celebrities.

He was ably succeeded by Joe Cloutier, Tony's long time aide. Joe was brilliant, principled and didn't make decisions until all options were exhausted. By that time, all his subordinates were exhausted as well. But Joe was almost always right. Those who knew him well loved him. I count myself fortunate to be among them.

John Cooper's stint as President was short, but effective. He brought the first outsider's view to management and, I thought, did an excellent job. John has the distinction of being the only person to serve as president of the four most prestigious oval tracks in the country...Ontario, California, Indianapolis and Daytona, where he is now. That's a long way from being an untitled employee of USAC at its inception.

Tony George, grandson of Tony Hulman, has impressed us all with his grasp of both the spirit and the mission of the Indianapolis Motor Speedway. He has many of the appealing qualities of his grandfather and a better grounding in the sport of auto racing. He's learned fast and his future is bright. Unlike his grandfather, if he makes a mistake it will probably be as a result of moving too fast, but that is youth and besides, things have changed. Tony George is the right man at the right time in my opinion, as indeed were his predecessors.

When you have good "bosses", the job is a lot easier. I've had the advantage of four of them in my twenty-year "watch." When you have a good team, it gets still easier, to the point where I sometimes believe my job is reduced to making sure I don't screw it up making the so-called "major" decisions.

I remember right after I was appointed Chief Steward in 1974, I was interviewed by the press. They asked me what I wanted to accomplish most. I told them my goal was that in five years, no one would know the name of the Chief Steward because there were no more controversies. How little I knew. Now, I realize there will always be controversies at the Indianapolis 500, no matter how efficiently it may be run. There's just too much money and too many careers riding on the outcome. So be it. It comes with the territory.

A Checkered Past

1. 1974: Of Headlines, Helmets and Hotdogs

"I felt the need for a strong motivation, a real desire on the part of the drivers to make this a successful start and a successful race."

The headline in the *Indianapolis Star* dated January 19, 1974 read "Binford New '500' Chief Steward." It's not every day that you learn about your new job in the daily newspaper, but that's what happened in my case.

After the 1973 Race, which saw three fatalities, a two-day rain postponement, and a great deal of negative press, the Speedway management felt that a change was needed. The first hint I had that a shake-up of the officials might be in the works was in mid-1973. I don't remember his exact words, but Tony Hulman, President of the Indianapolis Motor Speedway, asked me something along the lines of would I be interested in helping out at the Race. I said, "sure," having no idea that he meant "helping out" as Chief Steward.

Several months after that conversation with Tony, June Swango, his secretary, mentioned to me that Tony had been talking about making some changes, and wanted to know if I was available. She never said the words "Chief Steward," and offered no details, so I didn't think too much about it.

On the Hot Seat

I was certainly no stranger to the sport or the Speedway at that point in time. In fact, my first race was in 1935 when Kelly Petillo won. I was with my family in Grandstand A, and I remember that a woman behind us was drunk and threw fried chicken at us. Some things just don't change at the Speedway!

In 1954, I was one of ten men who got together, rented a car, hired a driver, and entered the "500." Shortly before the first day of qualifications, the car blew an engine, and blew our chances for a qualification attempt. The following year, three of the original group of ten bought a car. My company, D-A Lubricant, agreed to sponsor that car, driven by Cal Niday, Bob Sweikert, and Johnny Thomson, for four years.

USAC (The United States Auto Club) was formed in 1955, and I agreed to sit on the Board. I was elected President in 1956, and served in that capacity until 1969. From 1969 to 1974, I was involved in international racing, but remained on the USAC Board of Directors.

By 1974, I had been a steward at several Formula One races, but never a Chief Steward. Because of my involvement in USAC, I was not an unknown to the drivers, although there was one driver quoted as saying that he'd just as soon Dick King (President of USAC) be Chief Steward because he was used to working with him! Dick had more hands-on experience than I, but there was a feeling that the President of USAC shouldn't be on the firing line.

Until the *Star* article, I didn't realize that I was the one being considered for the "hot seat". In fact, Tony Hulman never actually spoke to me about the position. The Chief Steward is an employee of USAC, not the Speedway, but of course Tony had the right to veto USAC's choice.

I've always thought that the headline might have been a trial balloon. Ray Marquette, who wrote the story, never would tell me where he got the information. I figure he probably called the Speedway, didn't get a "no," and thought the probability of me getting the position was high enough to go ahead with the article. To this day, I'm not sure I would have gotten the job without that newspaper story!

After the *Star* piece appeared, Al Bloemker, Director of Media Relations at the Speedway, called me up and asked if I would take the job. I said I'd think about it, but definitely wouldn't unless they built a separate, elevated Chief Steward control center.

It was my feeling that my predecessor, Harlan Fengler, was handicapped by having to remain trackside throughout the race. The noise, the confusion, and the poor visibility of the track made officiating the race extremely difficult.

Lack of communication was another problem. The officials and observers around the track did not use two-way radios. The only way Harlan knew what was going on was if somebody came up to him and yelled in his ear—then he had to go to the telephone and listen in on the observers.

I was appointed only 60 days before the race, not enough time to make many personnel changes. I did make one. I added Art Meyers as a Steward and Chief Observer. He has been my right arm ever since.

A Spirit of Cooperation

Other than improving the communication at the Speedway, my main goal that first year was to try to create a climate among the drivers that would motivate them to drive the "500" both safely and competitively. This philosophy was nowhere more evident than in the official policies for that year where I told all the officials that we weren't the drivers' enemy—we were there to protect them from illegal or unsafe competition.

The racing fraternity felt that the media's massive reaction to the 1973 Race wasn't good for the sport, and I tried to convey to the drivers that we all have some responsibility to provide "a good show" for the fans and for each other. I said, "You all know that you can't win the race the first time around, nor is there any sense in taking chances on the first lap when there are still 497.5 miles to go. You're supposed to be the best in the world. So show me that we can **all** do it right to make it happen, not just most of us, or some of us."

I think the heat on the event from 1973, plus an approach of reaching out to the racers went a long way toward improving the race in 1974. My attitude was "we're in this together, what can I do to help you get through the start safely," instead of "you guys need to do your job better."

Furthermore, I have a mysterious theory that what happens on the track often depends on the frame of mind the drivers are in when they get out there. If they think the race is going to be conducted in such a way that they can run the best race they can, then they're more relaxed, and that contributes to the success of the race. My job, like that of a coach, is to instill an attitude that will serve the team well. I sensed that, prior to 1974, that kind of atmosphere didn't exist, which may have been the source of some of the problems during the 1973 Race.

Changes

There were a couple of decisions my first year that I felt went a long way toward creating a spirit of cooperation with the drivers.

The first was our official decision not to tow or push a car that was out of fuel beyond the north chute. Seven drivers objected, because they wanted to be towed all the way back to the pits. Our feeling was that it would just prolong the yellow light. They argued that if the car was towed back to the pits, at least they'd have a chance to re-fuel and get back in the race.

We compromised, and agreed to send tow vehicles (small tractors) to pull them in until Lap 190. After that, they were on their own until the race was over. From a safety point of view, it was a little more dangerous, but it was in the best interest of competition. Solving that problem was a good example of how you can either prove who's boss and say this is the way we're going to do it, or you can re-think it and, in this case, end up with a better way of handling it.

Another change made during my first year as Chief Steward was the introduction of a five-minute warm-up period 30 minutes before the race. The team managers and chief mechanics requested this, pointing out that if the weather was cool, the engines would not have time to warm up during the parade and pace laps. The Speedway had to agree, since the warm-up period would take place during the opening ceremonies of the "500." They did, I did, and so we arrived at another solution that recognized the drivers' needs as well as our own.

A third major change in 1974 was lining up the cars so that the rows were 100 feet apart instead of 50 feet as had been the case in previous years. This encouraged less bunching up ("packing up") at the start which in turn helped decrease the probability of a chain-reaction collision.

We also decided to take the pace car off the track at the exit of the fourth turn, which allowed the polesitter to come down the main stretch to the start at a higher rate of speed.

The Speedway made quite a few physical improvements to the track before my first year as Chief Steward. The pit lane was widened, the pits themselves were enlarged from 30 to 40 feet each, and adjustments were made to several retaining walls. All the improvements contributed greatly to the safety of the track.

Protests

Not to say that my first race wasn't without its share of hassles! The "energy crisis" of 1974 affected the entire country, and the Speedway was no exception. To save fuel, instead of four days of qualifications, we had four "sessions" of three and one-half hours each. The sessions were held on two Saturdays, and practice was eliminated during qualifying.

The irony was that Indy Cars used alcohol as fuel rather than the gasoline that was in such short supply. Still, to the public, there was no difference, and since all the other tracks that did use gasoline were cutting back, the Speedway followed suit.

The four qualification periods were further reduced to two by rain, however, the rules of qualifying remained the same. For example, one rule stated that all cars must be in line *at all times* during the qualifications period to maintain their position. In other words, as long as they are in line at the start of qualifying, every entrant will have one qualifying attempt to make the pole.

Johnny Rutherford and Al Unser, Sr. arrived late at the qualifying line and lost their original place. I enforced the rule, and, as Johnny wrote in his *Foreword*, they lost their chance for the pole. What Johnny didn't say was that when he came in to my office later to "discuss" the matter, he slammed his helmet on the floor for emphasis! He had been a friend of mine since his rookie days, but he didn't speak to me for awhile after that. We finally broke the ice a week later when we were both waiting to be interviewed by Sid Collins (then Chief Announcer of the Indianapolis Motor Speedway Radio Network). Johnny was cordial like the gentleman he is, and went on to win the 1974 Race, so our relationship didn't suffer any lasting damage (right, Johnny?).

I don't like having drivers upset, but when you have a rule that is so clear, what can you do but enforce it? What I didn't realize at the time was that it had never been enforced before!

The only other major controversy that occurred during May, 1974 was the protest by five teams who were left in line when qualifying closed on the last day. Once a field is established, there is no extension of qualifying time. The rule in this case was the same as it had been for ten years, and in the interest of fairness, I had to apply it to all drivers.

One rather humorous incident occurred during

that first race. I was up in the Chief Steward's booth hard at work when the phone rang. I picked it up to hear someone say "We need more hotdogs at stand 47."

My reply should have been "Sorry, we've got all the hotdogs we need out on the track."

I never met with Tony Hulman before my "rookie" race, and I never had a performance review afterward. I figured that no news was a high compliment! David Mannweiler's column appeared in the Indianapolis paper two days after the 1974 Race with the headline, "Nobody Thanked Tom Binford." I didn't need any thanks. When you've had a good race, you know you've had a good race, and thanks aren't necessary. The race did receive compliments in the press and from the fans. We were back on the right track and all felt very good about it.

It's difficult to relate today the challenge that first race brought and the tension it created in all of us. To the racing fraternity and the Speedway, "success" was a must, and all of us were under the gun in a sense. As the visible "point man," I probably was on the hottest seat, but there were many involved in the accomplishment. I just took one step at a time and prayed a lot!

On the day before the 1974 Race, however, the tension was starting to get to me. The Saturday afternoon before the Race, I left the track at about five o'clock in the afternoon. Nobody was home, so I took a nap, and experienced my first nightmare... in technicolor, yet.

I dreamed I was on the track, and everything was going wrong. There were fires and crashes all around me. I was sitting in the pace car in the fourth turn when the race started, and then began wandering through the infield as the chaos continued. I woke up in a cold sweat...but strangely relaxed. The worst had already occurred, so I quit worrying about the next day's race and got a good night's sleep. Still, I think I summed up the experience of my first "500" as Chief Steward best by what I wrote in Donald Davidson's *Indianapolis 500 Annual 1974.* "When the race was over...I felt like I was going to dissolve. I was probably the only one present happier than (winner) Johnny Rutherford."

2. Playing by the Rules

The life of a Chief Steward is limited to four or five years. After that time, he will have penalized too many people, and race drivers never forget.—Joe Cloutier (the late President of the Indianapolis Motor Speedway).

*In most cases, the penalizing for or prevention of infractions is not against a competitor; it is **for** all the competitors. (We) are their protection, not their adversary.*—Officiating Policies and Procedures, 1974.

The Chief Steward is to the 500 Mile Race what a referee is to a basketball game—both try to ensure that the contestants play safely and within the rules. The difference is that in the "500," 33 lives are involved. There is a much greater likelihood of severe injury if someone doesn't play fair, to say nothing of the millions of dollars and careers that are at stake in this once-a-year event.

I have found that non-race fans are unfamiliar with the term "Chief Steward." One evening in Florida, I was introduced to an attractive young lady by a hero-worshiping race fan as the "famous Chief Steward from Indianapolis." She didn't seem to be overly impressed, but I persevered in our conversation, until she finally asked me what cruise ship I worked for!

The Chief Steward's job is to apply the rules governing the running of the 500 Mile Race universally and fairly. To help me in that effort, there is a huge network of observers posted at intervals around the track whose job is to watch for rules violations (infractions). It's difficult to make judgement calls at 200 miles per hour, so no penalty is applied until there is independent confirmation. The most recently scheduled improvements will be stationary cameras in the four corners of the track with monitors in the Chief Steward's booth. This gives us replay capability should we need it.

Penalties Before 1974

In the years before 1974, it seemed penalties were rarely called. I was an innocent in that regard because I noticed that there were no penalties applied, but I thought it was because there were no offenses!

Of course, penalties were rarely called because there were no infraction observers, no radio or TV communications, and no confirmation of violations. The Chief Steward was down on the track without information, so how could he know if there was an infraction or not? Even now, with our system of observers and sophisticated communications, I've been told there were violations when there weren't, so it's no wonder Harlan Fengler didn't have any confidence in the reports he received.

What penalties there were usually occurred when one car passed another under the yellow flag. The black flag, which tells the driver to come into the pits immediately, was almost never used. I can remember one instance in 1963 when Parnelli Jones had words with Eddie Sachs because Sachs said that Jones' car had leaked oil on the track during the race, causing Roger McClusky and Sachs to spin. Jones was leading the race at the time, but in Sachs' opinion and mine, he should have been black-flagged regardless of his position

A similar situation occurred when A. J. Foyt was leading the race in 1974. His engine began to smoke as he came through a turn. Several offiicials reported it. Jack Beckley, the Technical Director, took a look and confirmed it as well. We black-flagged Foyt, who came in, obviously angry. Before we could adequately check the problem, he returned to the track, only to come in again on the next lap with a blown engine.

I believe we did the right thing by calling Foyt in, and we were subsequently proven right. If we had been mistaken, it would have been more than a little embarrassing. There is no way to take back an inappropriate black-flag penalty, unlike a one-lap penalty, which *can* be reversed.

A Different Style

I believe the drivers were surprised at the emphasis on rules that began in 1974. I like to think that the rules restored a discipline to the "500" that has stood it in good stead through the years.

A rule applies to everyone. There are 33 cars out there, and what we do to one car affects all the others. Helping one driver will hurt another, so we might as well do what's right and fair.

It's easy to get carried away and think you shouldn't apply this penalty or that one because the driver couldn't help it, or he's a nice guy and didn't mean to do it. That kind of thinking is dangerous, and once you start, it's a slippery slope down into favoritism. In other words, you can't do a favor for one entrant without doing a disfavor to 32 others.

The White Line

Occasionally, there is a rare exception when it is unfair to a driver to apply a penalty. An example of this was the "white line" rule in 1989.

In late 1988, there had been a change in elevation of the surface of the track between the safety lane and the track itself. This change in surface, marked by a white line, alerted the drivers that they were driving in the safety lane.

The function of the safety lane was to provide an area off the main track where a driver could go when not maintaining racing speed. The rule stated that, while driving on the track at a normal speed, a car's wheels must not drop below the white line onto the safety lane.

When the track was re-surfaced in late 1988, there was no longer a transition between the track and the safety lane, and the surfaces of both were identical. It became very tempting to drive "below the white line", if for no other reason than to take a short-cut around the track. It quickly became evident from the number of cars that violated the rule that it was going to be very difficult to enforce, particularly in heavy traffic.

My judgement was to abandon the rule, but Joe Cloutier had a very firm opinion that we should strictly enforce it. This was one of the rare times IMS expressed an opinion on a rule enforcement. I believe the reason was that the Speedway had created the problem with the track repaving.

After hours of discussion, I rewrote the rule allowing considerable leeway. Joe finally accepted it and we issued a special bulletin allowing use of the safety lane in emergency situations, but forbidding four wheels under the line during a qualifications run. The latter worked fairly well. We had only one disqualification.

Allowing use of the safety lane in emergency situations was a disaster. One driver claimed that his definition of an "emergency situation" was any time he drove through a turn! Unfortunately, his remark set the tone for the whole month.

Race day was another story entirely. Of course, we had discussed the white line situation with the drivers endlessly during the month, and none of them liked it. I kept telling them to trust me, and they kept asking me if I was going to penalize them. Finally, I said to just stay above the line as much as possible. If they had to go down there, they could, but continuous violations would draw a penalty.

From the drivers' point of view, they weren't getting any information out of me except that it's a rule, follow it, and you won't have to worry. That wasn't really fair to them. Some of them definitely drive better down there, and not driving down there could affect the order of their finish.

On Race day, during the first 25 laps, many cars used the safety lane legitimately, but others probably did not. I remember Al Unser, Jr. complaining about Michael Andretti driving under the white line, when Al had been reported on the same lap for the same infraction.

Before the 1989 Race was over, there were 1700 calls of white line violations—10% of the total number of turns made by every car in the Race! By the 25th lap, it was evident to me that the infractions were coming so fast, the Race wouldn't be over until dark if we penalized them all. It would have been an act of kindness to stop recording the incidents, because the poor guy that was writing them up had 15 legal pad pages full and wrote non-stop for three hours. I just couldn't bring myself to stop him because he was so engrossed in what he was doing. He just kept showing them to me, and I kept asking him if they were confirmed, knowing there was no way to confirm them because he couldn't call out for all the calls that were coming in.

No penalties were applied that year for white line infractions. The rule was unfair and impossible to enforce—what if a driver dropped below the white line because otherwise he would crash? Would it be fair to penalize him in that instance?

A four-to-six foot strip of grass now separates the safety lane from the track, making it impossible to drive down there. In addition, speed bumps have been added to the surface below the white line as another preventative.

Since 1989, there have been no further bulletins issued on the white line rule.

A Technique to Being Fair

As officials, we can be fair without being mean by concentrating on the offense rather than the offender. We consider ourselves servants of the race. If we can change a regulation that proves to be helpful to the field, then we try to do so.

The great pop-off valve controversy of 1979 was a case when a rule needed to be changed and was, but unfortunately, the timing of the change could have been much better.

The pop-off valve limits the amount of "boost" the turbo-charger produces. The ideal scenario as far as the driver is concerned is to keep the pop-off valve from "popping off", or opening. When the valve opens, it decreases the engine's horsepower and the car's speed. Our rule stated that every car's pop-off valve had to be set the same so as not to give any car an advantage. Any tampering with the valve in an attempt to increase speed meant immediate dis-qualification of the car.

In the middle of the second Saturday of qualifying, the cars driven by Dick Ferguson, Steve Krisiloff and Tom Bigelow, which had already qualified for the field, were disqualified. The reason given was tam-pering with the waste gate exhaust pipe which had the effect of overriding the pop-off valve, thereby illegally increasing the turbo-charger boost.

All three cars appealed and the appeals were denied on the basis that the wast gate exhaust pipe had indeed been tampered with. Still, after meeting and talking, looking at valves and really researching the rule, we concluded that the rule wasn't totally clear. What we really meant by tampering was that if the exhaust pipe was smaller than the standard pipe, 1.470 inches, we would consider it an illegal attempt to override the pop-off valve. We issued a bulletin to that effect.

I thought that re-defining the regulation was a great idea until 7 am the next morning when I began to get complaints that we had changed the rules in the middle of qualifying. The entrants who had been eliminated from the field objected that if they had only known the exhaust pipe had to be a certain size, they would have changed it before their qualifying run, and the results might have been different.

We had a hearing that went until midnight and we ruled against the protesters. But I talked to the then President of USAC, Charlie Brockman, and said that the disqualified cars did tamper with the exhaust pipe, so I had to rule against them. On the other hand, a case could be made that specifying the size of the exhaust pipe was actually a new rule that was made in the middle of qualifications and therefore not fair to those who had qualified legally and been bumped before the rule took effect.

In our defense however, we deliberately picked a size of the exhaust pipe that made everyone who had already qualified legal, except for the ones who had obviously grabbed a piece of metal, stuffed it in the exhaust pipe and welded it there to reduce the size of the opening. Where we ran into trouble was with those who had been bumped and claimed they might have been able to go faster had they been running under the "new" rule.

There was a line in the entry blank that said that the Speedway can do just about anything in the interest of the Race, and I felt that this might be an appropriate time to use it. We talked to the Speedway, and the decision was to allow seven bumped cars to have one attempt to qualify for the "500." Any car that went at least as fast as the slowest car in the current lineup could start the Race in the rear of the field.

We ended up with a qualifying session the Saturday morning before the race. Art Meyers was officiating the qualifying runs from just north of the starting line, the drivers were gathering at the starting line for their traditional drivers' meeting, and I was in court dealing with one of the disqualified entrants who had sued to be reinstated. An unusual Saturday before the Race to say the least.

Billy Vukovich and George Snider became the 34th and 35th cars to start the 1979 Race, the first time since 1933 that more than 33 cars had started.

In the final analysis, the three entrants who tried to "cheat" might not have cheated if the rule had been stated differently to begin with. We tried to define the rule better, but it was interpreted as changing rules in midstream. Recognizing that fact, I tried to seek a solution that would permit the bumped cars to have a chance to make the field under the same rules that applied to the first 33. It worked. Thanks to the cooperation of the Indianapolis Motor Speedway, no further protests were filed.

Caught in the Act

My concern with rules is actually my concern with consistency and fairness—if a rule is there, it should be enforced. Sometimes the entrants are caught red-handed in violations, for example, when Jerry Sneva's qualifying run was disallowed in 1981. A metal bolt had been stuck in the pop-off valve so it would stay closed while the car was qualifying. When Jerry came back into the pits after his run, he slowed down, a mechanic jumped on the side of the car and pulled the bolt out. Although we couldn't see him actually pull it out, we had eyewitnesses who saw the mechanic put his arm back by the engine where the pop-off valve was located. We also had an eyewitness to a mechanic sticking the bolt in, but we weren't aware of that until the car had already left the line to qualify. The car was subsequently disqualified.

In 1983, we had to eliminate about 14 cars from the qualifiying line because the side pods (a part on the car that affects aerodynamics) were either smaller or larger than the legal size. The rule was clear, but with 14 of them involved, I can't help but think the word got around that they could pick up a couple of extra miles per hour with a different size side pod.

The drivers involved wanted to fix their cars while they were still in the qualifying line, but I felt that it wasn't fair to hold up the line and make legal drivers wait to qualify. So the offenders lost their opportunity to be first-day qualifiers.

In this case, and in all cases, allowing a correction without a penalty would have encouraged the entrant to cheat. If he got away with it, so much the better for him. If he didn't get away with it, he could still fix the problem without punishment.

Covering the Bases

Many of the rules at the Speedway have come about as a result of specific instances. My feeling is that it's better to keep the drivers from making an infraction than catching them when they do.

Still, I don't claim that every rule is precisely called. We have to use some judgement—if we discover an infraction by a driver who's already dropped out of the race, what's the point in penalizing him?

We try to stay ahead of the game. As bad as it is for drivers to be surprised on the track, it's worse for officials. We practice "what would you do if..." scenarios during the month of May so we won't be caught off-guard when something unusual does happen. The problem with being caught by surprise is that it's easy to look only at one side of the matter instead of considering all sides.

One instance of a rule arising from a certain situation occurred in 1991 when we penalized Mario Andretti for having all four wheels below the yellow line that marked the pit entrance lane. The first time he did it, we penalized him a lap. The second time, we black-flagged him.

Once a driver is black-flagged, it is up to the official to tell him when he may go back to the track. The problem with using the black flag is that as a penalty it's inconsistent as to how much time the driver loses. If he happens to go back out onto the track as a yellow light comes on, the time lost is much less than if he's released from his pit into normal racing conditions.

Of course the drivers prefer the black flag to a lap penalty for that very reason. Mario's crew used his black flag penalty to refuel and change tires so there was virtually no penalty at all! The rule book has since been changed to forbid maintenance during a black flag pit stop.

It is impossible to write a rule to cover every occasion, and sometimes we can't even if we want to. One of these instances happened in 1983 when Al Unser, Sr. and Tom Sneva were battling for the lead, with Al, Sr. in front. Al Unser, Jr. passed Sneva and stayed between his father and Tom, blocking Tom from passing. Up in the Chief Steward's booth, we all watched it happen. Everybody thought it was wrong, but there's no regulation against blocking, and it was obvious that Al was doing it for his father, not for his own benefit.

As each lap went by, I kept thinking that this time, surely Sneva would get by Al, Jr. Finally he did, and went on to win the Race. In fact, Sneva said later that Al, Jr.'s blocking didn't really bother him, he was just waiting for the right time to pass. Still, it wasn't fair to Sneva.

Al, Jr. did come in to see me after the race, and admitted that he was just trying to help his dad. I told him that it didn't look too good, but I wasn't going to penalize him because he didn't do any harm. If I had penalized Al, Jr., it would have meant that I had to penalize every driver who blocks another. It's best to stay away from those unique kinds of calls.

One thing I don't do is scold a driver. Usually the situation speaks for itself, and I don't like to waste goodwill by scolding when it doesn't do any good. They are grown men, and I respect them, even when I don't agree with them.

Help Not Hassle

A private drivers' meeting is held on the Thursday before the race, and it is the most thorough meeting of the month. We discuss race procedures and any regulations they may want to question. It's called an "orientation" to distinguish it from the traditional drivers' meeting on the day before the Race. I decided in 1974 that the latter meeting was more show business than an effective dialogue with the drivers.

Sometimes there are questions about towing. My reply is that we will tow a car that has run out of fuel, but not after the 190th lap because it might interfere with the end of the race. Often a driver will want to know what the penalty is for a certain offense. In other words, what does it cost to cheat? My answer to that is don't do it and you won't have to worry about the penalty.

Although the entrants receive written bulletins about all rule changes, the danger of the drivers' meeting is that, if they're all talking at once, the drivers may think they've heard something different from what the rule says. I try to go over everything before they leave the meeting to make sure we are all in agreement. There are occasions when it's evident that they haven't read a regulation. It's my problem if they don't read them, but it's not my fault. If ignorance were a defense, I'd never be able to apply a penalty!

The drivers' meeting is a forum, and I try to convey the impression that we are listening and take their complaints seriously. I make it clear that we are there to help, not hassle them. We want to ensure a safe and fair race, and we appreciate their help in that regard.

Being fair doesn't mean we can't be sympathetic to the driver—what it does mean is that sympathy must not prevent us from applying the rules.

I can't be a public relations director and Chief Steward at the same time.

3.   It's Raining in Terre Haute, It's Raining in Clermont...

The decision to call it a completed race when rain occurs is based on three factors; the weather reports from the airport, the knowledge of the time it will take to dry the track after the rain stops, and the belief that when the strong probability occurs that the race cannot be resumed, the decision should be made and announced promptly—Chief Steward Report, 1976.

If it had not rained for three Race days in a row in 1973, Harlan Fengler might still be Chief Steward. Granted, the three fatalities and the tremendous negative reaction of the media played a huge role in the disastrous outcome of the 500 that year. Still, it was the ever-present wetness, combined with the decision to re-run the Race three days in succession without a break, that in my opinion was the basic cause of most of the problems that occurred in 1973.

The Third Time Is Not Always a Charm

Even before I knew I was going to take over as Chief Steward, I concluded that a serious mistake had been made in running the race three days in a row. One postponement is bad enough, although it's possible to run the next day without too serious a breakdown in morale and concentration. However, as was demonstrated in 1973, nobody could handle the third day. Not only had tension increased and morale deteriorated, but the grounds were a mess and a lot of people who were working at the track as volunteers had to go back to work, leaving the Speedway with much less manpower.

Which is why, when we were rained out on Sunday and Monday in 1986, I pushed for moving the third attempt to the following Saturday. Running the Race the next week-end would solve the problem of volunteer workers having to return to their jobs, and I wouldn't have to rely on a skeleton crew of officials. Also, everyone, including the drivers, would have ample time to rest, and the Speedway would have a chance to clean up the grounds.

Fortunately, the Speedway management agreed with me and we did schedule the 1986 Race for the next Saturday. It was a bit scary though, particularly when the third day was gorgeous. I couldn't help but think we were going to look pretty silly if it rained on Saturday!

We ran the 1986 Race on the following week-end with no sign of rain, without major incident, and it had all the feel of a first-day race. I wouldn't presume to claim divine intervention—we were just lucky. It also took the cooperation of the Milwaukee promoters, who had an Indy Car race scheduled the next week-end.

Calling the Race

If the weather is questionable on Race day, we have a hot line to the Weather Bureau at the Indianapolis International Airport. Sometimes they'll even call us and say it's raining in Terre Haute, or it's raining in Clermont, and we know it's coming. The Weather Bureau can tell us a front is coming through, but they can't tell us precisely when or whether it will hit the track.

Usually the drivers will know first if it's starting to rain because they see it on their windshields. Often, the rain will begin as sprinkles in the third turn—we call that "moisture" , which is one step ahead of "rain". The question then becomes should we turn on the yellow light and hope the "moisture" goes away after a few laps, or will it turn into a shower, causing us to stop the race.

I remember the 1975 Race ended in a downpour with no warning at all. Billy Vukovich spun on a soaking wet track in the fourth turn. When he returned to the starting line, he ran up to us and angrily asked, "Why didn't you turn on the red light when it started raining?" Art Mcyers, Steward and Chief Observer, replied, "Billy, have you ever seen a red light at the Speedway?" At the time, the red light system had not been installed, and Billy admitted that no, he guessed he never had seen a red light on the track!

It's not unusual for there to be different weather conditions on different parts of the track, so we always try to get confirmation from more than one observer whether there's moisture or rain. If it's just a little sprinkle, we'll often throw the yellow and hope it goes away. We did that for Rutherford in

1976, but ended by finally having to call the race after 102 laps.

I know the Speedway got barrels of mail after the 1976 race from fans who thought we should have restarted when it cleared up later in the afternoon. As I recall, it started raining at about 1 pm, and the Weather Bureau told us the rain would last all day. We'd completed at least 100 laps, which is the minimum distance required for a complete Race.

The Race was actually won in the pits under the red light. We were under the red light with 98 laps to go, and the rain stopped long enough to dry the track in the groove. The Weather Bureau told us it was going to rain again. We had to either decide to let the field go out and have a sprint race, knowing it would probably rain in about ten laps anyway, or wait around for it to rain and call the Race then.

I waited, and let the rain call the race. We knew the weather was coming, and to go out there and have a mad dash for a few laps to see who would win was not in keeping with what the Indianapolis 500 was all about. I felt it was best to go ahead and call the Race then instead of wait around until 6:00 and then call it.

Of course, the sun came out at about 4:30, but we still had at least two hours of drying time ahead of us. Conceivably, we could have re-started the race at 6:00 and gotten 100 laps in before dark.

That raises an interesting question—when is it too dark to race, and on which lap do we call the race? If we know it's going to get dark before the Race ends, which driver do we pick to win it? After all "too dark" is a moving target, not very precise. We would have to pick a specific time.

Needless to say, I wouldn't want to be put in a position to have to make those kinds of decisions, and so far, I've been lucky enough to avoid it!

In general, I think the public dislikes a shortened race because there is less to see, and the second place finisher dislikes it because he might have won if the field had gone the distance. As far as the winner is concerned, I don't think Bobby Unser in 1975 or Johnny Rutherford in 1976 felt "cheated" because they didn't win a race that went 500 miles. I always felt though, that Gordon Johncock got less satisfaction and less credit for winning a shortened race in 1973. It wasn't fair, but I believe that Gordy never really felt like he won the 500 until he won it the second time in 1982.

Delay and Postponement

The fans don't like a delayed race, but I don't think anybody objects if it gets to be 4:00 and we postpone the Race until the next day. Postponing or not postponing can be a question of ethics—is it ethical to start a race that's supposed to last 500 miles when we know it can't possibly last that long?

I believe we shouldn't start the Race unless we know the drivers can go the full distance. The fans are always a consideration, but it's really USAC's responsibility to run a race that is fair to the competitors. It's not fair to the drivers to deliberately give them a 250 mile race instead of a 500 mile race.

The question comes up every time it rains, but postponement is not really my call. Tony George, President of the Indianapolis Motor Speedway, has the final word on when the Race will be held.

Personally, I'm always relieved when the Race is over, no matter what the reason. I'm not there to watch a race, I'm there to officiate a race. The fewer laps they run, the fewer problems we have and the less chance there is something will go wrong.

When they pass the 101 lap mark, the cry in the Chief Steward's booth is, "We've got a race, we've got a race." We know then, that even if it rains, we don't have to come back tomorrow to find our winner!

Rain and Qualifications

We've actually had more trouble with rain during qualifications than we have during the Race. In fact, it has rained 12 of the last 19 years during some qualifying session. If "pole day" is rained out, then the next day of qualifying becomes pole day. Although it has never happened during my tenure as Chief Steward, if all four days of qualifications were rained out, we would keep trying to qualify day by day until the Speedway determined time had run out and the track was needed for Race day preparations.

If there were ever a scenario where we couldn't get an entire field qualified before the Race, there is a rule that states that the Speedway can select the field any way it wishes. In such a case, we might suggest selecting past winners, past national champions, and looking at practice speeds to see who has been going fastest.

The 1974 qualifying period was unique. Qualifying was reduced to four three-and-a-half-hour sessions to be run on Saturdays only. Rain shortened those sessions even further. That gave rise to the protests by everyone left in line at the end of the last qualifying period who said they didn't have "enough time" to qualify. Actually, the drivers of all the remaining cars had passed up their first chance to qualify, which is the only one the Speedway guarantees. The field was full, and the rule is clear that when the field is full, no extension of qualifying time will be granted. It's not fair to those competitors who were ready to go when their time came to qualify.

Wet weather during qualifications can have a real effect on the strategy of two-car teams, especially if they want to qualify one car on the first week-end and one on the second. Rain can also help the teams with cars not ready to run—they have more time to work on the car if the weather remains wet.

The track is no place to be when it rains. The rumor mill works overtime, complaints run rampant, and everybody has his own idea as to what should be done. Anyone who's smart leaves the moment it rains, and returns when the track is dry!

Of course, I can't leave.

Drying the Track

During qualifications, when the track begins to dry after a shower we'll often take the first two drivers in line out to inspect. Upon occasion, we've let the cars run when the groove is dry, even though the rest of the track may be damp. There's only one car on the track, the driver knows where the dampness is, and he knows it's dry where he's driving.

The track usually takes one to three hours to dry, depending on the sun and wind. We start the drying process by driving all the trucks around and around the track. At one time, all the 500 Festival cars drove around to help dry, but to maintain control, we found it best to restrict the drying process to Speedway vehicles. Toward the end of the drying procedure, Charlie Thompson, Superintendent of the IMS grounds, calls out the mobile track dryers.

We (the officials) decide when the track is dry enough to go racing. We always consult with Charlie, but the call is ours. I ride around the track to inspect during qualifications, but not on Race day. I'm not about to climb 105 steps up to the Chief Steward's booth twice in one Race!

Incidentally, 1992 saw a real breakthrough in track drying. The IMS finally discovered what was causing the "weepers"—water forcing its way through the cracks in the pavement. They were a major problem when we needed a dry track, but now, fortunately, the weepers appear to be under control.

Weather and Track Conditions

Although drivers have been known to complain about track conditions, they are supposed to adjust their driving to fit those conditions. The track is never perfect, but it's much improved, particularly since we don't allow cars to drive with oil leaks—we black flag them immediately. I've heard many drivers say that in the last 10 or 15 years, the track hasn't deteriorated during the Race the way it used to, which is one reason we're having some exciting finishes.

In 1988, there were 14 yellow lights and eight crashes during the Race. The day was much hotter than normal, and there was a theory that the excessive heat caused the wings on the car to lose the force that actually pushes the car down on the track. When that happens, the car gets loose and the driver has to slow down. There were enough accidents during the 1988 Race to tend to confirm that theory.

The 1992 Race ran under temperatures that were much colder than normal, and a cold track provides less traction. Still, the drivers have to adjust to fit conditions, and if they don't, they'll lose control. One of the ways the drivers adjusted in 1992 was by not changing tires, since warm tires get better traction.

It's hard to generalize that the accidents during the 1992 Race were caused by cold weather. But even if they were, what could we have done about it? We can't call the race because it's cold...or hot...or windy. Sometimes we wish we could, but that's racing.

4. To Be One of Thirty-Three

Qualifications are the most strenuous aspect of May for the Chief Steward. He's down on the track in the middle of the qualifying process, and things happen that have to be dealt with immediately.

Many fans' first exposure to qualifications comes when they see the first car roar out of the pits for a chance to be 1 of 33 on Race day. A driver's attempt to qualify for the Indianapolis 500 is actually the end result of a series of screening requirements that the entrants must pass before they can get behind the wheel.

When entrants first come to the Speedway, they have to pass a series of safety checks before they're allowed to drive on the track. At this time, they receive their initial certification decal, which the officials place on the car to indicate safety standards have been met.

Before drivers can compete in Indianapolis, they have to complete at least 10 laps on the track at "racing speed." Then, after undergoing and passing yet another series of technical checks, they get a second certification decal, which allows them to attempt to qualify for the Race. After receiving the second decal, the crews can still make changes to the car, but they will face another technical inspection before the driver goes out to qualify, and no changes can be made to the car after that.

Lining Up

The night before the first day of qualifying, we hold a meeting for crew members of all entrants. I go over some of the qualification procedures, and thank them for cooperating (even if they haven't).

Our "selective" method for determining the order of qualifying is as follows. The representatives from each team have to stay in their seats until I'm finished talking. When I give the signal, they all rush down from the stands at once, line up and pass through a gate. No pushing allowed. Each team draws a little numbered ball from a box. The number on the ball is the driver's position in the qualifying line. Simple, yet effective and fair.

Before we had the random drawing, the system for deciding who qualifies first was literally "first come, first served." It was similar to standing in line to buy tickets to a rock concert or to get into the track first— a long line-up of teams waited to get into the pits. Pushing and shoving was not unheard of, and they often appeared at 5 am to get "a good spot." As they filed past, the entrants gave their names to the official, and that was the order of qualifying.

All the teams were supposed to come through a certain gate into the pits. I can remember years ago when Roger McClusky figured out how to get in through an alternate gate. As the officials stepped into the pits through the main gate, there was Roger, one step ahead of them!

Staying in Line

On the opening day of qualifying, the first 30 cars have to be physically lined up in the pits at 11 am. To avoid congestion, the rest of the cars don't have to present themselves to the line until their time comes to enter the final inspection area. If they don't show up then, or show up late, they've lost their place and have to go to the back of the line. This is what happened to Johnny Rutherford and Al Unser, Sr. in 1974 when they lost their shot at the pole. Then, however, we required *all* cars to be in line at the start of qualifying.

As long as the driver stays in line, he has one opportunity to take the green flag and qualify his car as a first-day qualifier. If his attempt fails, or he isn't ready, he goes to the rear of the line. Each entrant may make three official attempts, if there is time before qualifications end.

Often, there are cars in line who have not had one chance to make the field at the end of the first day of qualifications. They will still be considered first-day qualifiers, even if their first attempt occurs on the second day.

Every car is guaranteed one chance to qualify—what happens after that is up to them. In 1974, some teams claimed there had not been "enough time" to qualify due to rain and the shortened qualification sessions. In reality, the problem was not insufficient time. Those teams had passed up their original chance to qualify, and unfortunately the bad weather made it impossible for them to make another attempt before qualifying was over. We ruled against them.

What we guarantee is not an *attempt* to qualify but rather an *opportunity* to get out on the track. For example, in 1978, A. J. Foyt went out to qualify, took the green flag, but returned without qualifying, complaining that his pop-off valve wasn't working properly. We checked it and it was ok, but Foyt had to go to the back of the line because he had taken his one guaranteed *opportunity* to qualify. If a rabbit had run across the track or it had rained, forcing him to come in, he would have remained at the front of the line because those occurrences would not have been his fault. In this case though, he simply failed to qualify so to the end of the line he went.

Bumping

The 33 fastest qualifiers start the race. Their position in the field is determined by the day they qualify and the speed at which they qualify. On the first day of qualifying, if 15 cars make the field, the slowest car will be on the outside of the 5th row. The fastest car on the second day will be on the inside of the 6th row, and so on until 33 spots are filled.

No starting position is protected, but it's safe until at least 33 cars have qualified. After that, any car that goes faster than the first 33 eliminates or "bumps" the slowest car in the field.

Nobody is immune from bumping. It is even possible, although not probable, to bump the pole car if 33 cars end up going faster. In 1955, it was extremely windy at the track, and Jerry Hoyt won the pole over just 1 other qualifier. Back then, there was no guarantee of the opportunity to be a first-day qualifier. When the closing gun sounded on the first day, the remaining drivers in line were automatically second-day qualifiers, so Hoyt was protected from being out-qualified for the pole, even though he was only faster than one other car that day. In fact, he ended up being slower than nine other cars before the field was set!

Although it's nerve-wracking for the drivers involved, the bumping process can be exciting. In 1988, Gordon Johncock bumped Rich Vogler, who then bumped him back at about three minutes before the closing gun. Double bumping has occurred more than once, but a lot of things have to come together for it to happen. The line in front of Vogler had to be short so that after Johncock's run, he still had time to jump into his second car and qualify.

Incidentally, it is the car that's bumped, not the driver. Once bumped, the car is eliminated, but the driver isn't. However, the driver can't qualify another car while the car he has already qualified is still in the field. No professional qualifiers allowed!

Controversy

Tradition has it that the Chief Steward sends the drivers off for their qualifying runs. In order to do that, I have to be down on the start/finish line, and accessible to everyone. When a problem comes up, people with no vested interest and people with a tremendous interest all crowd around trying to change my mind or complain. It's a lot more unstructured than the Race, when I'm safely ensconced in my Chief Steward's booth high above the track with the door locked and phone communication only!

The days can be long, especially if it rains. There is more pressure on the drivers to get in to the Race than to win the Race, which is why there seem to be more disputes during qualifying.

One of the rules states that, in order to count as a qualifying run, the car's engine has to be running as it crosses the start/finish line, but it doesn't have to be in gear. In 1988, Pancho Carter crashed coming out of the fourth turn of the final lap of his qualifying run. He slid sideways down the main stretch and kept on going across the start/finish line. Even with that accident, his speed was still fast enough to get into the Race. Pancho's crew wanted to count it as an official run. I said they couldn't because the rule said the car had to cross the line under its own power.

Pancho could have argued that he was "under his own power," or how else could he have crossed the starting line. I said, "Pancho, we'll accept that run. Now let's get that car back to the garage and see if it passes tech inspection. If it doesn't, we'll have to disqualify you and it will cost you one attempt." That ended the argument. The car was so badly damaged by the accident that he couldn't even drive it back to the garage, let alone pass tech inspection!

As one driver can't qualify two cars, neither can the engine of a qualified car be used to qualify another car. In 1979, after Bobby Unser had already qualified for the number four position in the field in a Roger Penske car, the team used the same engine to try to qualify a second car, driven by Bill Alsup. They claimed it was an accident, but the rule still states that a team is supposed to use the same set-up in the race as in qualifying, and that can't happen if one engine is used to qualify two cars.

I told Roger I'd give him a choice. He could either withdraw Bobby Unser and let Bill Alsup stay in the field, or we could disqualify the second car. Of course he kept the number four position and Alsup was out.

The Hurtubise Incident

Perhaps the most bizarre incident that has ever occurred during qualifications was when Jim Hurtubise decided to take a stand in 1978. On the last day of qualifications, he planted himself at the front of the qualifying line and refused to move.

As a little background, Jim had not received his second decal to allow him to qualify, since he had not attained 180 mph during practice. This was the speed required to receive a final decal (sticker), and it was a safety rule. He was still driving a roadster, which had a front engine, while everybody else had switched to a rear engine car. As a result, the tire companies were not paying much attention to him, and I think he was frustrated with his own career and convinced that the changes going on with the rear engine car were not in the best interests of racing.

Jim had a terrible accident at Milwaukee in 1964 that resulted in major burns on his hands. The doctors told him that they couldn't restore flexibility to his hands, so what permanent position would he like them to be in? He replied that he wanted them to be bent so he could still drive a race car. What devotion to his sport.

He was a courageous, likeable guy, a good man and a good friend. Jim could also be hot-headed, but until 1978, there were no major complaints or incidents with the exception of one in Milwaukee after a race where he complained to the press about the start and criticized the promoter. He came to my office the next week and agreed that he shouldn't have said what he said, we held a press conference to clear the air, and that was the end of it.

At any rate, there was Jim standing at the head of

the qualifying line at 5 pm on the last day, and refusing to move unless we let him qualify. I told him we would have to remove him if he persisted, at which point he jumped into the cockpit of Bob Harkey's car, which was the first car in line. He finally left Harkey's car and the Safety Patrol escorted him away from the line. Jim then broke away from the patrolmen and ran out on the front stretch while Harkey's car was on the track trying to make the field.

Luckily at that point, two State Policemen showed up, and I asked them to get Hurtubise and take him back to his garage. After qualifications were finished, I issued an order excluding him from the Speedway until the Race was over.

Jim knew the rules, and he would never have gone that far if there hadn't been a tremendous amount of pressure on him. After I excluded him, I wrote a letter to his wife, expressing our concern, and asking for her cooperation in keeping him away from the track so there wouldn't be any more incidents.

Jim never showed any anger toward me personally. I had a real reason to exclude him because I was afraid he would do something similar on Race day and cause injury to himself or others. It was sad to see a great driver and a great guy get to the boiling point.

All drivers react to the pressures of qualifying for the Indianapolis 500 in different ways, and it bothers some more than others. In contrast to Hurtubise, I remember one year when it had been raining during qualifying, and Jim MacElreath was first in line. The weather cleared, and when I came up to start him off on a qualifying attempt, he was asleep in his cockpit. Now that's cool!

5. "Go Green"—Starting The 500

The most important ingredient of a safe start, and indeed a safe race, is the conduct of the drivers—Chief Steward Report, 1974.

The start of the Indianapolis 500 is like no other auto race. As 33 cars come charging down the main stretch, the odds seem awfully long...like trying to roll a seven for the fourth time in a row on a craps table. I can remember the moment the field crossed the starting line during my first Race as Chief Steward. I pried my eyes open, and sure enough they'd gone by!

Since 1973, there has been almost a mystique about the start of the "500." It's become the culture to be concerned about it. The veterans talk to the rookies about it, and I talk to all the drivers constantly in meetings. I try to convey to them what they all know anyway, that where they are in the first two-and-a-half miles has absolutely no bearing on where they're going to be 500 miles later.

The 1973 Start

As I pointed out earlier, the start was by no means the only thing that happened to make the 1973 Race a disaster. Still, the accident at the start in the front stretch involving Salt Walther, 11 other cars and injuring 11 spectators seemed to be the one aspect of that Race that received the most attention. In my opinion, the cause of that accident may have stemmed from Walther's inexperience with the operation of the turbo-charger. The turbo-charger kicks in when the car attains a certain speed. If the driver isn't ready for it to engage, or isn't alert to the speed he's going when he accelerates, there is a burst of energy, and he can lose control. I think that's what happened to Salt Walther in 1973, and perhaps Kevin Cogan in 1982.

Also contributing to Walther's accident was the narrow distance between the rows. Fifty feet separated each row of three cars—not nearly enough distance to react and brake before impact.

Changes in the Start Since 1974

From the point of view of safety, widening the distance between the rows from 50 to 100 feet was our most significant change. The drivers gained twice as much time to react to trouble on the track, and the farther apart they were, the less likely they were to hit each other.

We also started taking the pace car off the track earlier. Prior to 1974, on the last pace lap, the pace car came all the way around the track and then ducked into the pits at the last minute. In 1974, and ever since, the pace car pulls away from the field in the third turn and goes down on the apron in the fourth turn. The front row then has a clear view of the track and also knows in plenty of time that they will be coming down the stretch for the start.

One of the changes we established in my first Race was to have a private drivers' orientation meeting on the Thursday before carburetion practice. We review the start in detail there, again at a meeting with the front row drivers, and yet again at a Rookie meeting

We expect the drivers to be in racing gear (125-130 mph) by the time they pass the starting line. We tell them they should start gradually accelerating when the pace car leaves the track after the last pace lap. The key word is "gradual"—they shouldn't stay at 90 mph and then suddenly floor it to 120 mph.

Nor should they stay at 90 mph all the way to the starting line! There's an advantage to the polesitter in bringing the field down the main stretch slowly. He knows when he's going to step on it, the field doesn't, and so he can perhaps get a jump on the rest of the pack. If all the cars are in racing gear at the start, their speeds are fairly equal, and there's a better chance of maintaining their positions in the field.

The problem with the pole position car bringing the field down slowly is that the cars tend to bunch up. In 1982, it was my feeling that polesitter Rick Mears came down the main stretch for the start too slowly. I don't know why. The rest of the cars were beginning to jockey for position, and Kevin Cogan lost control, taking A. J. Foyt, Dale Whittington, Roger Mears, and Mario Andretti with him. I think people assumed that it was Cogan's fault, and he probably took more punishment than he deserved.

In all fairness to Mears, he has led the field from pole positions many times and done it very well indeed. He did a great job on the "restart" in 1982.

Preparing for the Start

We probably discuss the start with the drivers more than any other single aspect of the Race. First, there's the private meeting with the three qualifiers on the front row. I'll talk to the polesitter one-on-one if absolutely necessary, but I really prefer talking to all three at once. What's important is not just what they say to me, but what they say to each other.

We talk about where on the track we drop the green flag—about 200 yards before the starting line opposite the old pit entrance. The importance of maintaining a straight line is also discussed, as well as the polesitter's right to start the Race. In other words, the pole position car should cross the starting line first. After that, he's on his own.

One of the most common questions that comes up in the front-row meeting is what gear does the polesitter intend to be in when he crosses the line. That is my cue to tell them the speed they should be going coming out of the fourth turn (80-90 mph) and the speed they should be going by the time they start.

During the private drivers' meeting on the Thursday before the Race, I tell them to drive defensively. The wind and suction in turn one is difficult to handle. There's a lot of turbulence at the start, the front tires lose traction and the car doesn't handle the way it normally does. A driver has to pay attention to make sure he gets across the line and through the first turn safely.

The Race is not won on the first few laps, and it certainly isn't won when the cars cross the starting line. In fact, the drivers really shouldn't think of the race starting until they reach the back stretch on the first lap—what they're doing until then is keeping out of trouble.

The Field Takes Off

The progression of events leading up to the start of the Indianapolis 500 is precisely timed. We have an official assigned to every two rows of cars, who's job it is to make sure that every driver moves along on time. For example, we may notice that a driver in Row Six still isn't in his car when everyone else has already climbed in. We'll say to the row official, "Row Six, can't you get that guy to move any faster?"

The reply, "Well, he's having trouble with his helmet."

"He should have started adjusting it earlier, push him if you can!"

It's a wonder we can ever get 33 drivers into their cars at the same time!

After the command, "Gentlemen, start your engines," the pace car and celebrity cars take off and the front row begins to move. The celebrity cars complete the parade laps, then exit, and the pace car driver takes over for the final pace lap. One of the best celebrity pace car drivers was James Garner. He drove the pace car in 1975, 1977 and 1985.

After the start, the celebrity pace car driver's job is finished, and our own driver takes over. Don Bailey has done the job in recent years and done it very well. In addition to the driver, there is a steward in the pace car with radio contact to the Chief Steward's booth. Bob Cassaday, and recently, Rich Coy, have served in that capacity. It's a tough, thankless job!

As the field takes off, if a car does not have its engine started, the rest of the field passes on by. If the car is still not moving by the time the field has come around the fourth turn, the driver must come into the pits for safety. Once he gets started, it's our judgement as to when we let him go back out on the track. If the rest of the cars were in the backstretch on the final pace lap, we'd hold him until the race has begun. On the other hand, if the field were going into the second turn, we would probably let him go to the rear of the pack. We tell the other drivers to leave a hole for the one who's having trouble—don't close up because he may be able to get back into position before the start. We would not let him try to regain his position in the field unless it could be done on a parade lap. It's too upsetting and can be dangerous to have a car working its way through the field on the pace lap.

Two officials, a rider and a driver, are in the pace car. They are in constant radio contact with Steward Keith Ward who stands next to me. The pace car receives precise instructions, right down to the speed it should be going on each warm-up lap. On the parade lap, it should be going about 50 mph, then move up to 60-70 mph on the first pace lap. By the time the pace car is ready to leave the track, it will be going about 80-90 mph.

The pace car has flashing lights on when it's out on the track. When the pace car is ready to leave the track prior to the start of the Race, the lights are turned off before the third turn so the field knows the car is going in. Once the pace car commits itself to go into the pits, it must do so. However, in 1986, Tom Sneva had an accident after the pace car's lights had been turned off, but before it had pulled in. The lights went back on, and the pace car had to stay out there.

We have told the drivers that once the pace car goes in, assuming that there are no problems, they'll get the green flag. I'm on the phone with the starter and say, "go green." We turn on the green light, located at intervals around the track, and the starter waves the green flag simultaneously.

Deciding to Start

It's my call whether to start the Race. If it looks like an unfair or a dangerous start, then I wouldn't give the green flag. Luckily that's not happened yet during my time at the Speedway.

The only year I've come close to not starting was in 1990. In my Chief Steward's Report of that year, I called the start "an artistic flop and a technical miracle. The front rows were bunched after the green flag dropped and other rows strung out. I almost didn't call for the green, but thought that would be more dangerous under the circumstances."

Most of the time, starting is not a hard decision to make. The field looks very ragged when it first starts out, but each row of drivers can't get in line until the row ahead of them does. By the time they come around on the first parade lap, they should be lined up. However, a lot of them are still warming their tires up at that point, so we don't actually require them to be in rows until the pace lap.

All we can expect is to have the front of the field in reasonably good order by the time we go green. If the first five or six rows are in good shape, then I don't have to worry too much about the remaining rows. By the time the rear of the field comes to the starting line, either the field has begun to sort itself out, or all Hell has broken loose!

No one observer can see the whole track, but I do get reports from observers posted around the track and there's always the TV monitors. The monitor on the back stretch is particularly helpful.

I don't feel the pressure to start the Race as much as I feel the pressure of the consequences of not starting it. For example, if the field is not in order just before the start and we can't go green, the drivers must line up behind the pole car without a pace car. At that point, the cars in front are beginning to slow down because they know we're not going to start. Other drivers in the rear are way back in the fourth turn, may not realize it's a non-start and are still racing. In a case like that, it's an invitation to disaster if you don't give the green flag.

Maybe it would be a disaster if we did start, but that's the judgement I have to make. I would lean toward a slightly sloppy start rather than a re-start.

The important thing is that it be as fair and safe a start as we can make it. The goal we're always trying to reach is for the drivers to cross the line in the order they qualified. Every driver out there has the capability to be precise if he wants to be. However, it only takes one who doesn't want to be, the others get nervous and try to make up the advantage they think he just gained. Then we have a potential mess.

Crossing the Line

I define a safe start to be everyone crossing the starting line without incident. If anything's going to happen, it's probably going to happen before the first turn. By the time the field is into turn one, they should be in a better position to avoid a multi-car accident.

Part of the cause for spins and crashes before the start is that the field is so close together, which affects the aerodynamics of the cars. However, the drivers are also nervous, which might have something to do with the problems we've had before or immediately

after the start of the "500." Notice I said "before" or
"after", not "during." Given my definition of a safe
start (and it is my book!), we've only had one accident
during the start since 1974, and even that one can be
argued!

In 1986, Tom Sneva crashed on the parade lap
before the start, and Josele Garza's spin in 1987 was
in the first turn after the start. Scott Brayton spun in
the second turn of the first lap in 1988, and Gary
Bettenhausen lost control in the first turn after the
1991 green flag. Roberto Guerrero's spin in 1992 was
on the pace lap, again before the actual start.

Kevin Cogan's crash on the main stretch in 1982
probably came closest to being a "bad" start. However,
when he lost control, the green flag had not yet dropped,
so the accident was still technically before the start!

The Ideal Start

If I could start the "500" any way I chose, I would opt
for 33 cars in single file. From a safety point of view, it
would be ideal. However, that will most likely never
happen because the last car would be down a lap before
the Race ever started. My second choice would be two
abreast. I think it would reduce the odds of an accident
by 50%. However, three in a row is so traditional at
Indianapolis that it would be very difficult to change.

We tried once to change—we started the parade laps
from the pits. The cars came out two abreast, and then
were supposed to form the usual rows of three. The front
row ended up ahead of the pace car! They didn't actually
get into their proper positions until about 100 feet before
the starting line.

That was before my time. I hope I wouldn't have
started the Race under those conditions, but who knows?

Shaky Knees

My knees shook the first time I started the Race, and my heart always starts beating faster when I hear *Back Home Again in Indiana*. At that point, I know the start is just minutes away and the excitement is building, even for veteran officials.

Still, the success or failure of the start is ultimately up to the drivers. I'm not driving the cars myself, and it's probably a darn good thing!

O.K., A. J., let's see your fireproof bodysuit (1974).

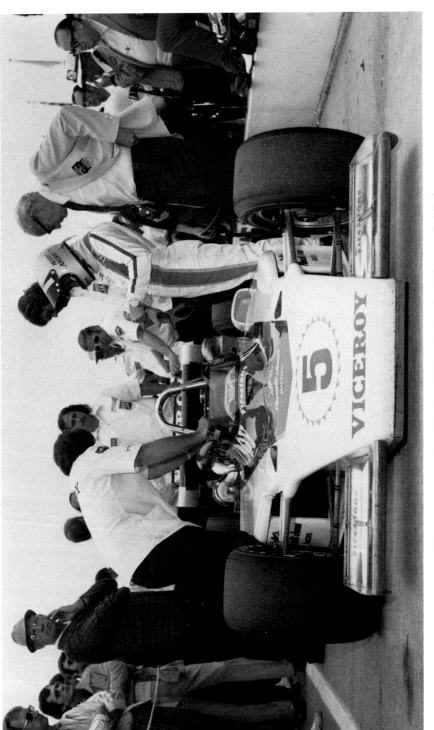

Tom takes one last look at Mario Andretti's car (1974).

Tom Binford shares a light moment with Tom Bigelow (1976).

Bobby Unser and Tom (1976).

Tom and Tony Hulman (1976).

The Chief Steward speaks at the 1977 Drivers' Meeting.

The "cool", calm Jim McElreath gets last-minute instructions from Tom (1977).

A young race fan requests an autograph (Tom swears it's the only request he ever got) (1981).

Mario Andretti and Tom—a "respectful" discussion (1986).

A. J. Foyt and Tom share a thoughtful moment (1986).

6.   *The Run for the Checkered*

"At the Indianapolis 500, (anything) is possible. If you can eliminate or avoid potential catastrophes, you will be successful. This takes experience, steady nerves, and attention to both detail and attitude. Maybe even more than that, it takes luck, if not divine intervention."—Chief Steward Report, 1980.

I spend the night before the Race on a fold-out couch in the Indiana National Bank suite at the Speedway. The track is virtually empty, except for two trucks who do laps all night for security. There's always a rumble out on 16th Street, but other than that, it's quiet...the proverbial calm before the storm.

The sun or the crowd wakes me up. If I'm awakened by rain, then I'm not nervous because I know the Race is going to be delayed. After breakfast at the Speedway Motel, I get to the track about 6:30. Unless there's a problem, I have nothing specific to do until 10:15, when I climb up to the Chief Steward's Booth. Before then, it's just waiting, waiting, waiting...but not waiting alone. There are hundreds of people in the pits and it seems most of them come by my spot at the starting line to say hello. I doubt if I'm very good company, particularly if they're looking for an extended conversation. The pressure begins to build.

I'll never forget a Race day morning when one of the yellow lights would not come on during a final test about 30 minutes before the green flag. That's probably the most nervous I've ever been! Thanks to Charlie Thompson's crew, the problem was diagnosed and corrected with a few minutes to spare. All Race mornings are tense, but some are more tense than others!

One of the Chief Steward's official duties has always been to make a track inspection shortly before the Race. It's not really necessary, because the safety trucks always inspect the track again later, but it's tradition. I believe it was started years ago to make sure all the gates were closed so cows wouldn't wander onto the track! It still seems that every year, there's a rabbit or a dog we have to chase away.

Binford's Army

On the morning of the Race, while I'm busy waiting for a crisis, about 300 officials and volunteer workers are taking their places at various points around the track. Observers are posted, and technical people and firemen are assigned to their pits. There is one certification man, a technical inspector and two firemen for each pit, plus one additional fireman for every two pits.

The technical inspector's day actually begins early in the morning in an entrants' garage, where he ensures that the team plays by the rules. I don't think the crews have ever been too pleased with his attentiveness, although it's extremely rare that the technical person ever catches any violations. During the

Race, the technical inspector's job is to watch for any infractions while the car is in the pit, such as tampering with the pop-off valve or using dry ice to reduce the volume of fuel in order to fit more into the fuel cell (tank).

He must also watch for infractions such as crews getting out in the pit lane too soon before the pit stop, too many crew members going out to the pit lane or drivers running over or hitting equipment. The cars are not inspected immediately before the Race due to time constraints, but the first ten finishers are always inspected afterward, along with any other car that we may suspect of a violation. If we find an infraction after the Race, the entrant could be fined, or at worst, disqualified.

However, the difference between getting into the Race and not getting into the Race is much more significant than finishing fifth instead of thirty-third. Frequently, sponsorship contracts hinge on making the field, so qualifying for the Race means big money to the participants. Therefore, if we're going to see "bending" of the rules, it will tend to happen during qualifications rather than during the Race.

While the technical inspectors are in the pits before the Race, the Timing and Scoring workers are in the Tower Terrace testing their equipment. Their job is to monitor the speed and lap time for each car. The final result of the Race is contingent on their records, so not only do they have a computerized system, but there are also 33 people keeping track of each car the old-fashioned way—with a pencil and a stop-watch!

Each car has a small radio or "responder" fastened to it. Whenever the car goes over timing strips that are buried in the track, a signal is sent by the responder to the computer. In this manner, we know where the car is on the track at all times, which lap it's currently running, and what current, past and average speeds are.

In years past, we couldn't post the Race results until 8 am the next morning because Timing and Scoring had to reconcile' their multiple systems. Beginning in 1993, we'll post the finish at 7:45 pm the same day, thanks to the responders and the computer.

Getting the Facts

My job during the Race is to administer a system I hope will give me the facts about what's going on in terms of infractions. I leave the monitoring of the competition to Timing and Scoring, who do a tremendous job under the direction of Art Graham and Les Kimbrell. The Chief Observer stays constantly informed about what's going on around the track—he probably sees the Race less than anyone else because he has to pay attention to what the observers at their posts are telling him.

Infractions come in to the Chief Steward's booth via headphones. Before I take any action, I check with Art Graham's Timing and Scoring people to get a confirmation from more than one source. I can also talk to an observer directly if needed.

If we determine that there has indeed been an infraction, we notify the team in person as soon as possible after it happens so they can take it into consideration as part of their Race strategy. We probably could call them on the radio, but we want the message delivered by an official steward so they can respond.

I remember at one point during one of my earlier Races, Dick King, current President of USAC, was up in the Chief Steward's booth with me. A driver had committed an infraction and we were still in the process of confirming it when he came into the pits and was subsequently out of the Race. Dick leaned forward and said, "Tom, sometimes if you wait a little bit, problems will go away." I'd rather wait awhile before calling an infraction, as long as there's no danger involved, than call one too early and have to retract it.

Yellow lights are usually called by the observers, so the only two decisions I need to make are going green or going red. Even at the end of the Race, Art Graham from Timing and Scoring tells me who get's the checkered flag based on his time and speed records, so I just have to make sure the starter displays the flag to the right car! Duane Sweeney, Chief Starter, hasn't missed yet, so my job is simple. Watch Sweeney do his.

We all watch the Race with our ears rather than our eyes, because we can't see the whole track. That will change beginning in 1993 with the scheduled addition of four stationary cameras around the track. It's hard not to watch when the drivers come down the front stretch, but we usually don't have time because we have other things to do. Sometimes, when we go 30 or 40 laps with out a yellow light and there are no infractions at the moment, we can watch the Race, but those times are rare.

TV Coverage

In 1986, we had the first live network TV coverage of the Race. It permitted us to have a monitor in the booth, which we could use for re-runs if we needed to. It would have been nice to have that option in 1981, when we didn't know about Bobby Unser's passing infraction until after the Race was over. (Unser was penalized a lap after the Race and the victory awarded to Mario Andretti. After hearings, Unser subsequently regained his win and was fined for the violation). I understand Jackie Stewart played it up quite a bit on the delayed TV broadcast when it happened, but nobody from ABC ever called to tell us about it!

We recognize that the TV people need information. They have wanted to station one of their people in the Chief Steward's booth and we've resisted that, but we have set up an open telephone line for them to ask questions during the Race. Mike Miles stays on the line the entire Race and passes ABC questions on to me.

I don't know if it makes that much difference whether there's a broadcaster in the booth or not , but there's an old saying that if people knew how they made bologna, they'd never eat it. Maybe that applies to officiating, too!

Closed Pits

The closed pit rule and pit speed limit that began in 1992 were two of the more dramatic changes to the running of the "500" in the last twenty years. We wanted to close the pits (forbid the drivers to come in for a pit stop) for at least one lap after the yellow light came on. This would discourage the lead cars from speeding up to get into the pits, when in fact they were supposed to be slowing down under the yellow.

Closing the pits also caused a quicker pack-up, or line-up behind the pace car when the yellow light came on, and made it easier for the pace car to pick up the correct leader. The drivers had no incentive to race to the pits, since they couldn't enter until the pack-up was secured.

We debated the closed pit system a long time, and let a lot of people know about it to get preliminary reaction. We finally decided to try it in 1992. There was some fear that by packing the drivers up under a closed pit rule, there would be a mad dash for the pits when they re-opened, and mayhem would result. In fact, no more than one lap ever went by before we opened the pits again, so there was no need for any panic pit stops.

Along with the closed pits, we also enforced, for the first time, a speed limit in the pit lane. The system was made up of a series of timers with large monitors that would show the speed of each car while it was entering or exiting the pits. The idea was that the officials could see the monitors and so could the drivers. The drivers knew their own speed, and also knew that if they were going over 100 mph, they had to slow down.

We now have timing strips in the pit surface to transmit the speed, but in 1992, we used radar guns and the monitors didn't work! One radar gun did record the speed at the beginning of the pits where the drivers could see it. However, we didn't find out until the first yellow light that the speed was recorded but the monitors weren't showing it!

The drivers had no idea that we didn't have a clue how fast they were going in the pits. They all followed the correct speed beautifully, just as they were supposed to do, thinking of course that we were watching them closely. It was the biggest bluff we ever pulled, and we'll never get away with it again!

The reaction of the drivers to the closed pit rule was mixed at best. We had been talking about it for three years before 1992, and many were opposed to it.

The drivers complained, "What if we run out of

fuel, what if we have a flat tire, what if we have a mechanical problem and can't get into the pits?"

I replied, "Well, what if you crash in the first turn? That's not our problem, it's your problem. You can come into the pits but it will cost you a lap."

"But it isn't safe to be out there in a car with something wrong with it and not be able to come in."

My answer was, "If it's not safe, then come on in to the pits. We never told you to drive an unsafe race car, in fact, we black-flag cars that aren't safe."

After the Show

I'm never sorry when the Race is over. I leave the Chief Steward's booth as quickly as I can and cross the track before the winner goes out for his victory lap. I head straight for my office, and there I stay, waiting for information and any complaints. The observers have to turn in their reports, Timing and Scoring is trying to get the preliminary finish out and the technical inspectors are busy going over the first ten finishers' cars and any other cars that require it.

Occasionally, I'll go back to the garages and congratulate the winner or somebody who did well, or somebody who should have done well but had some bad luck. There's not a whole lot I can do in an official capacity until the results are posted.

After the official results of the Race are posted on the door of the Steward's office in the Tower Terrace, I stay in my office if somebody needs to come in to explain or complain. The teams have an hour after the official results are posted to file a formal protest. We haven't had a formal protest hearing for a long time, but there have been many informal ones. Almost every year, there has been some crew whose records do not agree with ours—they'll come in and compare notes, and 99.9% of the time, we're correct. Of course, the one tenth of a per cent of the time we're wrong can be pretty major as we saw in 1981. But that's another chapter!

If I get involved in an informal protest and the allowed hour is almost up, I'll always warn them that time is growing short, so they better get their protest in writing to me right then. Usually, the teams are coming in not to argue, but to find out what mistake they made, especially if there are penalties applied after the Race.

After the protest period is over, we have a meeting of all the key officials to review the Race and make recommendations for improvement.

Memorable Races

In 1987, Al Unser, Sr. won his fourth 500 Mile Race. It was a case where experience triumphed over equipment, as his car had a year-old chassis and an old Cosworth engine. Still, Al had enough sense to know that the only way he was going to win the Race was if the cars that were faster than his would drop out and he would be there at the end. If it didn't happen, it didn't happen, but if it did, he would be there. That's the way he thinks and that's the way a smart race driver thinks.

At the "500," most agree the race car and crew are 75% of the equation and the driver is about 25%. It's an important 25% though, and I think Al Unser demonstrated that. He knew he couldn't make the car do what it couldn't do—he had to accept what he had and go on from there.

One of my more satisfying Races occurred in 1986. It was the first time since 1973 that we had been rained out twice in a row. We ran the Race the following Saturday, there were very few yellow lights or accidents, the officials and the fans came back, and we ended up with a good Race.

When Bobby Rahal won in 1986, he was not part of the racing "establishment"—he had come from the Sports Car Club of America rather than from midgets and sprint cars, which was the classic way to get to the Speedway. He's always been a consistent driver, smart on the track, and not pushing his equipment to destruction. He's much like Rick Mears in that respect.

The 1992 Race was bizarre for several reasons. It was one of the coldest Race days in recent memory. The combination of cold tires and a cold track probably contributed to the 85 laps run under the yellow. It was also the closest Race in history, with .04 seconds separating the winner, Al Unser, Jr., from second place, Scott Goodyear.

Although it certainly appeared that Unser and Goodyear were neck-and-neck at the end, according to the responders in both cars, there was about a half car length between them. In horse racing, it's called a photo finish, but in auto racing, the whole integrity of the system is based on time.

For example, what if we took a picture of the finish that showed a different result than the finish times? The responder is not located in the nose of the race car, and until 1993, the rule did not state specifically where on the car the responder had to be. What would happen if the responder on one car were located two or three feet in front of another car's responder? It would be possible to take a picture that looked like a car won when, according to the recorded time, the car came in second because its responder was located in the tail! The rule now states that the responder must be located in approximately the same place on every car.

Another close finish occurred in 1982 when Rick Mears and Gordon Johncock were dueling at the end. I think Mears let Johncock intimidate him, and I'll bet Mears himself would say he should have "gone a little deeper in the turn." He certainly learned from it, because when Mears was running with Michael Andretti in 1991, he didn't let Michael bluff him out of that one—he stood on it and won the Race.

Everybody in the Chief Steward's booth gets tense when two cars are running together, because we know if something goes wrong, it can be disastrous. However, if everything goes right, we're just as excited as the next guy. After all, even officials can be race fans!

We didn't worry about Mears and Johncock. Good drivers are not out on the track to take risks, but they always recognize when it's necessary to take the risk to win. We knew that even though Rick and Gordy were going to take chances, they were always on top of what they were doing.

I used to hold my breath watching Johnny Rutherford—he would take chances where I didn't think the odds were in his favor, but he won three Races, so who am I to judge?

Races have been getting closer in the last 20 years. The number of pit stops and yellow lights tends to pack them up, so it's very difficult to get a lap lead. Still, it's hard to believe that after 500 miles, two cars can end up side by side at the end.

7. 1981—A Public Relations Disaster

For officials, the standard is perfection. We all must fall short. One thing is certain. If competitors ever thought rules infractions would be condoned or covered up for political or public relations reasons, they have learned differently.—Chief Steward's Report, 1981

The 1981 Race was a "public relations disaster" that might have been prevented if Bobby Unser had learned of his penalty shortly after it occurred instead of at 8:00 that night. It also might have been prevented if I had known about the possibility of a penalty immediately instead of 15 minutes after the checkered flag.

The facts were that on the 149th lap of the Race, which was running under the yellow light at the time, Bobby Unser, in third place, and Mario Andretti, the leader, came into the pits. They both left at almost the same time.

The rule for leaving the pits and rejoining the field which is packed up under the yellow was clear on paper. However, it wasn't so clear in the drivers' heads, at least, not until Bobby Unser's notorious infraction in 1981. It didn't help any that Bobby had missed the drivers' orientation meeting that year when we explained the rule again.

Our Side of the Story

The rules stated a specific procedure the drivers were supposed to follow when re-joining the field under the yellow. A driver exiting the pits at the time the field is packed up is to pick his proper place in the pack-up at the end of the pit wall. He then remains in the safety lane until he exits the second turn. At that time, he rejoins the pack in the place he would have occupied had he not gone into the pits.

In other words, he is not permitted to gain position in the field after he exits the pit. Bobby Unser, in his eagerness to catch Mario Andretti, passed six cars and therefore gained six positions in the pack...a major infraction.

We have had special infraction observers since 1982, but in 1981, we did not. Instead, we relied on the observers at the pit exit to determine where the exiting car was located relative to the pack-up. It was up to the observer at turn two to determine when the car rejoined the field.

Neither official alone could determine if an infraction occurred. Information from both observers was necessary, because the infraction doesn't occur until the car rejoins the pack out of position. If the driver who is exiting from the pits passes cars on the track and permits them to repass while he is still in the safety lane, there is no infraction. The officials didn't suspect a violation, and so did not communicate with each other or me.

TV knew it because they had cameras watching the whole thing. Shortly after the Race, I was in my office and got a hint that Bobby Unser passed an undetermined number of cars under the yellow.

We started an investigation. We checked what records we had, and also watched a replay of the television broadcast. There was some criticism later because TV wasn't an official medium, but it wasn't an unofficial one either. The regulations were and are mute on the subject of "official media."

Once we saw the TV delayed broadcast, there was no question in my mind that Unser had committed an infraction. The rule book permits us to apply penalties until the final Race results are posted—which, until 1993, happened at 8 am the next morning. The Chief Steward has traditionally reserved the right not to call a penalty after the Race if he so chooses.

However, from an ethical point of view, I didn't see how I could ignore Unser's flagrant infraction. I didn't have much difficulty, in spite of all that happened afterward, in deciding whether it was right or wrong. I was sure I was right in applying the penalty, and did not hesitate, even though I know if I had taken a vote among the stewards, it would not have been unanimous.

I've had a wonderful career in auto racing, but I haven't put my entire life into it. If I had, I might have been a little more hesitant about getting myself involved in political heat that had the potential to ruin my career. It was also a tremendous boost that the Speedway backed me up in my decision. I still don't know whether they agreed with me.

The great thing about Joe Cloutier, Tony Hulman, and now Tony George, was that when a problem arose, they didn't try to go back and second guess what might have happened. The Unser/Andretti

protest was basically a USAC matter, and the Speedway was only involved because they couldn't pay the
purse until they knew who the winner was. They
certainly were involved from a public relations point
of view, but officially, the Speedway has nothing to do
with applying penalties.

The Result

Although Bobby Unser did file a formal protest of his
one-lap penalty, the dispute never went to court.
Hearings were held within USAC in front of a three-
man panel. Since it was not a court of law, the rules
of evidence were not the same. In fact, in my opinion,
the three-man panel didn't have the authority to
change Unser's penalty, but that's what they did. The
verdict was a double-edged sword for Bobby, although he did regain his victory. However, the panel
decided he *had* violated the rules. A lap penalty, they
said, was too harsh, so he was fined $40,000 instead.

It was a great verdict (I didn't like it) from the point
of view of keeping everybody happy. Unser got his
victory, I kept my pride in doing the right thing, and
USAC got $40,000! Of course, Mario Andretti wasn't
very happy, and later appealed to both USAC and its
parent organization, the Automobile Competition
Committee of the U.S.

If Unser hadn't passed those cars, would the result
of the 1981 Race have been any different? At the time
he committed his infraction, he was running in third
and Andretti was in the lead. He regained the lead
shortly thereafter and held it, but began to slow down
on lap 198. When Unser received the checkered flag,
he was only 5.2 seconds in front of Andretti. It could

have gone either way, but the odds were that Unser would have won anyway.

I think the knowledge that Unser won the Race influenced the panel, and in my mind it shouldn't have. It was after the fact, and irrelevant to the infraction. As far as the change in penalty was concerned, the Rule Book was clear. A one-lap penalty was mandatory.

Looking back, I think much of the negative public reaction resulted not so much from applying the penalty, but from applying the penalty after the Race was over. On the other hand, if I had applied it on the 190th lap with the public still in the stands, there might have been an even bigger reaction. When the decision to give Unser a lap penalty was publicized, all the race fans had gone home and weren't as focused on racing.

I'm acting as though everyone was against my decision, but in fact, there were probably some people who said "It's the officials' job to make the call, they did it, and I accept it." Of course, those who felt that way were limited to family members, close friends and maybe a few employees!

After 1981, we did go through the rule book and rewrote a number of the rules. Among others, we established a non-protestable infraction which basically said a judgement call could not be disputed.

The majority of the drivers accept penalties. Both Mario Andretti and Bobby Unser acted like nothing had happened when I saw them after the matter was settled. I got the feeling, however, Andretti, while he wanted victory, wished it hadn't happened at all. It had to have been much harder on him to go for two months as the winner of the "500" and then have it all taken away.

So what's the big deal? The big deal was that a one-lap penalty after the Race had never been applied to an unofficial winner.

Would I do it again? Yes, but I hope I never have to.

8.   The Rookies

There are two types of rookies who come to Indianapolis. One is the true novice, who hasn't had much experience in an Indy Car and needs all the help we can give him. The other is the road racing champion or Formula One driver.

We tell them all that the Indianapolis 500 track is unique in the world, and if you don't respect it, it'll bite you.

Rookies don't come to Indianapolis "fresh off the turnip truck." To the fans, they seem to explode onto the scene during the month of May. In reality, the road to Indianapolis is long for a Rookie.

The best experience a Rookie can have before coming to the 500 is driving on the Indy Car circuit. Barring that, he needs to have participated in racing at speeds of at least 150 mph.

The midget and sprint car circuits used to be the source for nearly all the drivers at the 500 until road racing and Formula One had a revival in the sixties and seventies. All of a sudden, Rookies were coming to the track who had experience driving at fast speeds against other good drivers, but had never been seen at a midget, sprint or stock car race.

The good thing about midgets and sprint cars, is that they give a driver experience in wheel-to-wheel competition. There are not as many Rookies coming from that arena today partly because the speed difference between midgets and sprints and Indy Cars is so great today.

To be invited to the Indianapolis Motor Speedway, a Rookie has to have made a name for himself in other races. That's usually enough for the USAC committee to allow him an opportunity at the "500," but it certainly isn't enough for a car owner to "give him a ride."

The money and the sponsors are two things a Rookie must bring with him or her to get a ride at the Speedway. Racing is a business, and the owners are professionals. They'll rent the car, but the driver better provide the sponsor.

The driver can't just be a driver anymore. He has to be a salesman, a promoter and an agent for himself. Roger Penske has brought drivers to the 500 without sponsors, and some of the other teams have too, but the majority of the owners consider that they're giving the Rookie a chance to make it—in turn, he or she must contribute a sponsor.

The drivers who have already made a name for themselves in Formula One competition have a little easier time getting a ride at Indianapolis. I think we tend to have more foreign drivers here than we used to because of the high profile of the Formula One circuit, and the success of such road racers as Jim Clark, Graham Hill, Mark Donohue, Danny Sullivan, Emerson Fittipaldi, Bobby Rahal and Arie Luyendyk.

The Rookie Orientation Program

The Rookie Orientation program is about 12 years old, and was begun by Roger McClusky, former driver and Director of Competition for USAC. Although it's not required for the Rookies who want to come to the "500," it certainly helps them get acquainted with the track, the rules, and their car before the pressure of the month of May begins.

Roger McClusky, Art Meyers and I review all of the applicants for the program to determine if they have enough racing experience to come to the Rookie Orientation program. Drivers who need a refresher course can also apply. If they are accepted, the would-be Rookies are invited to the Speedway for a Thursday through Sunday in late April.

They spend most of their time running laps, demonstrating that they can drive a race car. Roger instructs the Rookies in rules and procedures, and they can also complete the first three phases of the Rookie Orientation test. During each phase, they have to run ten laps at certain speeds. The speeds increase each time a group of ten laps is completed.

If the drivers pass the first three phases of their Rookie test, they come back in May for the last phase. One reason for that is to be sure their test is "official", but a better reason is that the last phase is taken under the observation of a veteran driver, and it's hard to find them before May.

During the last phase of the Rookie test, the driver must run laps at better than 205 mph. The veteran drivers observe, and look for consistency and ease as the Rookie drivers are entering and exiting the corners. If they're consistent, the veterans will give them a passing grade. Sometimes it's better to have a newer veteran judging, because they have more empathy, having recently been a Rookie themselves.

The veterans judge the Rookies for two reasons. First, they're better at doing it simply because they're drivers themselves. Second, if the Rookie has been approved by a driver rather than an official, then the veterans can't say that the officials don't know what they're doing because they've never driven a race car!

A would-be Rookie generally knows when he's not making the grade. He'll often drop out because his crew can't get the car going, and we'll suggest that it might be better if he came back next year.

Usually, if a Rookie flunks his test, he doesn't come back. However, Eddie Sachs flunked his Rookie test the first time, and went on to become a well-known driver, so there's always hope!

Money means an opportunity for a Rookie test. We try to get away from it, but there's no way to restrict how much money can be spent on a car. One system that has been considered to equalize spending is a claiming race. In other words, a team could spend any amount they wanted on a car, but anyone could buy the car at the end of the Race for a specified price. It sounds like a perfect solution, for who would want to risk spending $1,000,000 on a car that could be purchased after the Race for $250,000? The problem is that nobody wants to give up secret ways of making a car go faster, and anybody who buys a car will know what those secrets are.

It's done in horse racing, but we've always concluded that a "claiming" system wouldn't be appropriate for the world's leading race, based in part on the world's leading technology.

Rookie Meetings

The Rookie meeting that we hold before the Race is the most important of the month for the new drivers. Unlike the other drivers' meetings at the Speedway, I'm just the facilitator at this one. My role is to make sure the Rookies understand the rules and procedures, but it's up to the veterans to share their knowledge as to what it's like to drive in the "500."

There are always at least two or three veterans who speak at the Rookie meeting, and we try to make sure that one of them is a second-year man who still remembers what it was like to be a Rookie. In past years, Pancho Carter, Al Unser, Sr. and Johnny Rutherford have been among the veterans who have given the "new kids" the benefit of their experience.

The start is the portion of the Race that seems to concern the Rookies most, and there are always lots of questions about it. The veteran drivers talk about the start, maintaining position and driving defensively. Al Unser Sr. always says that when the yellow light comes on, don't jump on the binders (brakes). He says that every year, so it's my guess that at some point, somebody must have done it to him!

The "old-timers" mention with regularity to the Rookies that "if you're about to be passed in the turn, don't move over. Hold your position, and we'll pick the spot to pass. If you do move over, there might be another car trying to pass you on the other side."

The experienced drivers also warn the novices about the suction that takes them into the first turn of the track at the start. They also discuss the importance of raising their hand if they're going into the pits, so that the driver behind them knows they're going in, and can adjust his line accordingly.

It's difficult at those speeds to see a hand, but if a driver raises it high enough, the guy behind him can see it. By the same token, if he raises his hand too high, he'll be caught in a 180 mph gale and throw his shoulder out of joint, which has happened, I'm told.

The veterans are motivated by safety and making sure the Rookies know what's going on, but they also want to make sure the Rookies are predictable. It's in the veterans' best interest! It's a safe bet that the Rookies can figure that out.

The meeting with the Rookies is important. I wish any fan and everybody connected with racing could listen to it. They would be encouraged by the veterans' sincere attempt to share what it's like out there.

The 500 is a pretty intimidating place for a Rookie, and for most of them, it's the high point of their career. Their concern in the meeting is genuine, and nobody is cocky. Al Unser, Sr. particularly has a knack for giving them the straight story—he'll kid them and say that they may think he's telling them all this stuff so he can "whip them out there", but everything he says is true. "Raise your hand, use your rearview mirror when you go into the turn, and don't jump on the binders when the yellow light goes on."

I always enjoy the meeting. In my experience, overall, we've had less trouble with Rookies at the start and during the Race than we've had with the veterans who think they know what they're doing!

Rookie of the Year

The criteria for the Rookie of the Year award is based on which Rookie performed best throughout the month of May. In previous years, it's seemed to depend on who had the highest finish, and there isn't any question that a huge part of the performance is judged by the Rookie's position at the checkered flag.

However, in 1984, we had three Rookies finish in the top five—Roberto Guerrero was second, Al Holbert was fourth, and Michael Andretti was fifth. Guerrero and Andretti were co-winners of the Rookie of the Year award. What about Al Holbert, who actually finished ahead of Andretti?

Although I'm just one of a committee of many who have input into the Rookie of the Year decision, I feel that overall performance is as much a criteria as performance during the Race. There could be many reasons why one Rookie who had been outstanding all month didn't finish as high as another—in fact, one long pit stop could make the difference. Although Michael finished below Al Holbert, he was the fastest Rookie qualifier that year, drove an outstanding Race, and that was all taken into consideration when deciding the award.

The committee who chooses the Rookie of the Year is selected from officials and the media. It might be more interesting if the drivers themselves voted the honor. Surely the decision of a jury of his peers would mean more to the Rookie of the Year than the current jury of sportswriters and penalty-happy officials!

Minorities at the Speedway

The first female driver, Janet Guthrie, arrived at the Speedway in 1976. The event was so newsworthy, that it was difficult for her to move through the pits with the crowd of photographers constantly on her heels.

Janet's presence was a media event, but she conducted herself well. I don't think anyone in all fairness could say that she was any different from any other driver in terms of how she drove the race or how she acted off the track.

Nobody could fault her for doing less of a job at the Speedway—in fact, she did a better job than a lot of them! As stewards, we wished her well, and I believe most people did. I certainly didn't think that there was much, if any, feeling at the track that there was no place for women in the sport.

When Lyn St. James qualified in 1992, she wasn't the first woman to make the field, she was the second, so she didn't experience nearly the press attention that Janet did. Lyn was well accepted and did an excellent job in the Race. Her poise was exceptional.

When Willy T. Ribbs came to the Speedway in 1985 as the first African-American, it was my feeling that he drove an ill-prepared car. George Bignotti, Chief Mechanic, had not had time to put his magic into the car. I think Willy knew himself that the car wasn't ready, and was wise enough to leave moot the question of whether he was.

He ran about 48 laps and that was it. As far as I know, he got out of the car of his own volition and I think he was smart to do so. When the car isn't prepared, it's foolish to get out there and try to run hard. The best thing Willy could have done for his career was exactly what he did.

When Willy Ribbs came back to the Speedway in 1991, things were different. He got up to speed in good order and qualified very well. Unfortunately, he dropped out of the Race very early with car problems. Hope he gets another chance.

Why haven't there been more African-Americans and women at the Speedway? I don't know the answer except to say that it's not the color of their skin or the color of their hair that matters, what it usually comes down to is the color of money—Rookies have to bring sponsors to the Speedway, and if they haven't achieved a high enough level of competition to attract a sponsor's attention, then they won't get here, no matter what their sex or race.

We, as officials, certainly can't play favorites with minority drivers and/or owners. However, we can welcome them when they come and do everything in our power to make their experience at Indianapolis a productive one. I believe they are good for the sport.

It's Not Easy Being a Rookie

It's becoming more difficult for a Rookie to "break into" the Indianapolis 500, and not just because of the need for money and sponsors. The careers of veteran drivers are much longer than they used to be due to the increased safety of the sport, which leaves fewer slots open for Rookie drivers. The road to Indianapolis is not as clear-cut as it was—no longer does a driver necessarily go from midgets to sprint cars to Indy Cars.

In choosing potential Rookies, we used to rely on the car owners, assuming that if they were going to trust their car to a driver, he must be ok. That doesn't work anymore, because now the owners are as interested in a drivers' ability to bring money to the team as they are in his ability to drive a race car. In deciding whether to invite a Rookie to Indianapolis, we try to talk to people who have actually seen him run, but that's not always possible.

The Indy Car used to be essentially the same car, but bigger, as those in the sprints. Now it's quite a change for a driver to go from a sprint to a championship car since the sprint cars are front engine and the Indy Cars have their engines in the rear. The Formula One Rookies have the advantage at the Speedway because their cars are similar to Indy Cars.

It would be far simpler to decide who is qualified to come to Indianapolis if we required a potential Rookie to have raced on the Indy Car circuit for a year. We haven't done it because it would tend to exclude international drivers.

It's not easy being a Rookie at Indianapolis. There are only 33 spots to fill in the 500, the competition gets more fierce every year, and a Rookie hasn't won the Race since Graham Hill in 1966. The previous Rookie of the Year winner, no matter how well he does in the Race, is not guaranteed a ride the following May—nor are some veterans. Each year is a new beginning at the 500 for most drivers.

9. The Winners

Unless you're an insider, it's hard to realize the importance of the Indianapolis 500 and the pressure on each driver to seek every advantage he or she can. There's so much money involved and so much reputation on the line. I know there have been times with all of the drivers in the past 20 years when they were hurt by something I did, or thought I should call something I didn't call. I hope they didn't hold it against me permanently. It's nothing personal. Officials have jobs to do, too, and even make bad calls now and then.

In all my years as Chief Steward, I've never had the Speedway tell me what to do. They make suggestions, but most of the time it's in reply to a question or problem I've brought to them. It's hard for people to believe, because of the power the Speedway management has, but they've never tried to influence my decisions.

I do remember one instance though, when Joe Cloutier, President of the IMS, came close to it. In 1978, during qualifications, A. J. Foyt (1961, 1964, 1967, 1977) flunked an inspection, we didn't let him run, and he lost his position in the qualifying line. All

103

of a sudden Joe Cloutier showed up and sat on the wall. He didn't say a thing, he just sat there. Just his presence—he *never* came down to the starting line—made people wonder what was going on. I went over to him and got a hint of why he was there. Joe was a Foyt fan, and wanted me to explain what had happened so I did. That was the only time I ever saw Joe come close to showing concern about the treatment of an individual driver, and Tony George has maintained the same "hands-off" approach. I'm appreciative of that.

Out on a Limb and Up on a Ladder

One of the most interesting confrontations with A. J. Foyt took place in the mid-seventies during practice one year when we decided to start enforcing the rule that drivers had to wear fireproof underwear (body suits) whenever they drove the car. We had been requiring them to wear it for qualifications and the Race, but not for practice.

A. J. came out to run some laps, and I told the officials to see if he had his fireproof body suit on. He didn't. We wouldn't let him get in the car.

Of course he was upset about it, and even went to the phone in the pits to call me to complain. He stomped around but he wasn't really Foyt-mad, he was just Foyt-acting up.

At any rate, he went back to his garage, then returned to his car a little later. He knew I could see him, and he had his collar buttoned up so nobody could see if he had his body suit on.

A. J. got in his car. I asked if he had the fireproof suit on.

He said, "I'm not going to tell you."

I said, "You're not going out in that car unless you have it on and we know you have it on."

He replied, "Aw, I am too."

I said again, "You're not going out in that car today unless you prove you're wearing the underwear."

"Aw, ok," he said, and pulled his collar down so we could see he had it on.

Even though it was a relatively minor point, there are some situations where I have to stand by my guns. The possibility exists that if I hadn't stood firm on that rule, Foyt could have gone out without the fireproofing, had an accident and gotten burned. It certainly wasn't a question of whether Binford with all of his rule books, penalties, fines and prohibitions could face down poor little A. J. Foyt who happened to be the greatest race driver in the world!

I know if I'd ever really tried to face him down, I might have won the battle, but lost the war...the public relations war, that is. I can see the headlines now, "Foyt Denied Practice Without Underwear, Binford's Sanity Questioned."

Normally, I wouldn't have even been a part of inspecting underwear, but Foyt wanted me involved because he knew I could change the regulation if I wanted to and the other officials couldn't. Besides, most of the officials were Foyt fans and they didn't like to tell him what to do so I had to!

A. J. and I had another "discussion" in 1978 early on the morning of the Race. There was a dispute as to whether the blower on his car had been improperly replaced. I told him over the phone that we weren't going to let him start unless he fixed it.

"Not going to let me start!" he said.

"Those are the rules," I said.

Foyt stayed in his garage. It was starting to get late, and still he hadn't brought the car out. Finally, with just about ten minutes to go until the engine warm-up period before the Race, the car came out with the blower properly installed. I didn't penalize him for being late, although I probably should have.

I gave in a little bit because I didn't want to take A. J. out of the race over something so small, but I wouldn't have hesitated to do so if it had been illegal. On the other hand, I'm sure Foyt is more important to the Race than I am as far as the fans and the promoters are concerned. Still, a race can be run without Foyt, but it can't be run without officials! A. J. does have the upper hand, though, because USAC can fire me but they can't fire him. He's irreplaceable.

Seriously, in resolving a dispute such as this or any other, fairness to all the drivers is the key. If it's not fair, even though it may be emotionally satisfying, it bothers me.

Although the title of this chapter is not "A. J. Foyt," he's the only driver who's been around the Speedway as long as I have. Longevity has its rewards, not the least of which is being the subject of a Chief Steward's reflections!

Around 1957, when I was President of USAC, I went to Dayton, Ohio to see a track that was supposed to have been re-paved the month before for a race to be run that day. The problem was that the promoter had re-surfaced the track too late and the asphalt wasn't hard yet.

When I arrived at the Dayton racetrack, the cars were running on the safety lane because the rest of the track was still too soft. It was obvious the track was in no condition for racing, but the crowd was there, waiting. Nobody wanted to tell the fans there would be no race, so I volunteered. Across from the starting line, there was a starter's stand with a ladder leading up to it. I climbed up, took the microphone, and gave the crowd the bad news. As I turned away to go back down to the track, who should I see standing on the ladder but A. J. Foyt and Eddie Sachs, even angrier than the spectators.

Foyt was in front and said, "What do you mean we can't race; we came all this way for nothing?"

I said, "It's not safe to race on the track, it's not even dry."

A. J. replied, "Well, are we going to get any money?"

I told him I would try. I doubt that they did get any money. Pity the poor promoter who had to tell A. J. Foyt and Eddie Sachs they weren't going to get paid!

A. J. Foyt has always been known as a hard driver, but he rarely takes chances when other cars are around. He might come awfully close to the wall during qualifying, but he knows he can do it. He's a prudent driver, which I think is the secret to his phenomenal success at the "500" and on the Indy Car circuit. I don't think he should retire—if I'm still here, he surely can be! Or maybe we both should retire...not a bad idea, A.J., how about it? I will if you will.

Mario Andretti (1969)

Mario has a way of running his own race the way he wants to do it. He attacks the track like a 25-year-old rookie, which is a very high compliment to him because he still has that drive. His passing techniques are certainly thrilling to watch.

Even after the 1981 Race, Mario has never lost his cool with me, although we have had numerous "discussions" over the years. Well, "never" is a pretty strong word!

As I mentioned earlier in the book, one year, Mario was indulging his tendency to drive consistently with four wheels under the white line in the fourth turn. That was still against the rules because it basically allowed the driver to take a short cut through the turn.

Mario wasn't trying to bend a rule, he was just driving his natural line. Natural line or not, we couldn't let him be an exception. I penalized him a lap the first time, and gave him a black flag the second. He let me know what he thought...respectfully, but firmly.

Bobby Unser (1968, 1975, 1981)

Bobby and I haven't always seen eye-to-eye, but he was a good race driver and does an excellent job as a color announcer for various races. He's intelligent, personable and I like him.

As much as the 1981 Race meant to him, he never confronted me and was always very pleasant. I think he knew I did what I had to do. He didn't bear a grudge—he won the appeal as far as he was concerned, and I won as far as I was concerned because they upheld the infraction call. Some people give Bobby a great deal of credit for retiring before I could get back at him!

Al Unser, Sr. (1970, 1971, 1978, 1987)

Al and Bobby have very different personalities. Al is quieter and not one to speak out in a crowd. He has a keen sense of humor, and is much more "laid back" than Bobby. Al is a very smooth driver, and is particularly good at sharing his experience with the Rookies at the Rookie Orientation meeting before the Race. In general, he keeps a low profile out at the track—until he wins the Race!

Al Unser, Sr. is undoubtedly one of the greatest natural Indy 500 drivers. I rank him with Foyt, Mears and Parnelli Jones.

Gordon Johncock (1973, 1982)

Gordon is an aggressive, good race driver. He's very much of an individualist—independent and doesn't go along with the crowd. He has gotten mad and come to me to "discuss" it, but he doesn't go to the press with it. Gordon is who he is, and doesn't put on airs.

As I mentioned elsewhere, I don't think the 1973 win, shortened by rain, meant as much to Gordy as his subsequent win in 1982. That victory came after a brilliant duel with Rick Mears on the final laps.

Danny Sullivan (1985)

I like Danny, and I think he won a remarkable Race in 1985 when he spun and still took the victory flag. I had some "discussions" with him about a penalty several years ago when he had a hard time accepting that he had passed under the yellow, but that was just racing "stuff".

Danny had success in racing very young. He drove Formula Two in Europe before he came to Indianapolis, and that's where I met him. He's a good driver, and I think he can win again if he has the right equipment. Danny's also a "heady" (smart) driver, and handles himself very well off the track.

Tom Sneva (1983)

Tom is a witty, clever, and personable guy. He's also a very fast driver. I like him, and was pleased to see him win in 1983. He's a great qualifier, and his reputation has always been that he could go as fast as the car could go, and maybe faster.

Rick Mears (1979, 1984, 1988, 1991)

When Rick won his first Race in 1979, my impression of him was that he was easy to get to know, personable, and an extremely smooth race driver. I was delighted that he won because he was a new face at the Speedway.

He hasn't changed after winning three Races since then. I would still describe him as a very nice guy. He never came in to me to complain or question anything, but just stuck to driving a race car. Rick was very easy to work with.

I don't know all the reasons he retired from racing, but I admire his courage in doing it, and not sticking around because he might win his fifth "500." It takes a lot of moral courage to decide not to race anymore when you could still do it and make a lot of money. I admire him for making the sacrifice it took to carry out his decision.

Johnny Rutherford (1974, 1976, 1980)

Johnny is a great representative of the sport. For example, every year, all the former winners of the "500" are invited to attend the Mayor's Breakfast before the track opening. I bet Johnny's never missed one, and sometimes, he's been the only former winner there. Johnny's presence at the Breakfast is good for the "500," and good for the sport in general.

Johnny won his third 500 Mile Race in 1980. On his way to Victory Lane, he picked up Tim Richmond, who was stopped in his car on the main stretch. Johnny gave him a ride down the pit lane. The gesture was typical of Johnny's personality.

Emerson Fittipaldi (1989)

We have had a number of "foreigners" who have driven well at Indianapolis during my 20 years, but none who have performed as consistently well as Emerson Fittipaldi. Nor have any fit into the culture of Indy Car racing with such ease.

The year before he won the Race, I left the Victory Banquet with him, and mentioned that I expected to see him in Victory Lane next year. I'm not a prophet, but I haven't forgotten that, especially because the same thing happened with Danny Sullivan!

Wilbur Shaw, three-time winner of the "500", used to say when asked who was going to win the Race, "That's why we run it...to find out." That's the way I find out. We officials don't speculate very much, but when we do, Emmo is a name that comes up often.

Al Unser, Jr. (1992)

"Little Al" and Michael Andretti were celebrities when they arrived in Indianapolis, partly due to their famous fathers, but also due to their first-rate performances. It would be normal to expect them both to be cocky or prima donnas, but neither one has ever caused any problems, either as rookies or since.

Michael has left the Indy Car circuit to try his hand at Formula One racing and I wish him well. I predict he will return some day to win the Indianapolis 500. He deserves to win and he's come close on more than one occasion.

Al, Jr. has been a joy to work with. He doesn't gripe, but he does communicate. If something seems wrong to him about the rules or the officiating, he speaks up in a respectful way and listens. Two incidents that took place with Al, Jr. define his character.

The first one was in his rookie year when he tried to help his father win by blocking Tom Sneva. It didn't seem to bother Sneva so I didn't let it bother me. What it showed me was an appealing loyalty to his dad and his willingness to demonstrate it at a considerable risk to his own fortune.

The second instance took place when he was running nose to nose to tail with Emmo in 1989. During an attempted pass for the lead on the 199th lap, they tapped wheels, causing Al, Jr. to spin. Some drivers would assume it was the other drivers' fault and exercise their temper. Not Al, Jr. He got out of his car and gave the "thumbs up" signal to Emmo as he came around on the next lap.

Bobby Rahal (1986)

Bobby Rahal came to Indianapolis known only as a road race driver. He had proven himself one of the very best road racers in the country, but that didn't cut much ice in those days. After all, the Indianapolis Motor Speedway was an oval...the most demanding oval in the world. It didn't take long for him to demonstrate his ability on ovals. He has not only won the "500," but has threatened to win almost every time he has participated. From the officials' point of view, he's a pleasure—intelligent, articulate and gifted with common sense.

I remember one year talking with Bobby the day after the Race and he calmly informed me that we had missed a call on a car passing during the yellow light. He didn't complain or even criticize. He just wanted me to know so it might not happen again. I believed he was right. As I recall, had we caught the infraction, Bobby might have improved his position. I admired his restraint.

Arie Luyendyk (1990)

During my time as Chief Steward, there have been only two foreign-born winners of the "500," Fittipaldi in 1989, and Arie Luyendyk in 1990. Many times foreign drivers have had some problems due to the language barrier and the difference in rules...not these two. They were on top of things from the beginning.

Arie always showed respect for the track. Many foreign drivers, especially the "stars", tend to underestimate the four corners at Indianapolis. After all, they are used to three or four times that many turns on the road racing circuits of Europe. They soon learn that the precision required for the "500" track is far beyond the precision required for a road race.

Arie understood this, took his time, and mastered it in short order. Always willing to sign autographs or visit with the fans, he is a credit off the track and on. I've never even had a "discussion" with him.

Gary Bettenhausen

Gary is an excellent driver. He's had some injuries that have affected him, but even as recently as 1992, he was running out there just as fast or faster than anybody else. I can't help but think that the only reason Gary has not yet won the "500" is that he's never had the best equipment.

I was close to Gary's father, Tony, who was the drivers' representative on the USAC Board when I was president. He was active on the drivers' behalf, and always stayed very much his own man. Gary is like him—he's opinionated, but never a complainer. I admire him for his devotion to auto racing.

Pancho Carter

For years now, Pancho has been very close to breaking through as a "500" winner. He's a very good, top-rated driver, and has represented the drivers on the CART Board. He also does a great job for us during the Rookie Orientation meeting.

Pancho's a smart driver. He can be counted on not to do anything foolish. I think with just a little luck, Pancho will get a Speedway victory.

Some Closing Thoughts

I've never been a race driver and I 'm not really a "race fan," but I 've seldom known a race driver who wasn't a winner. They come in all shapes, sizes, IQ's and even personalities, yet they all have a certain spirit, commitment, courage, and self-confidence.

I've truly enjoyed working with them. And when I say "them", I mean many more than are mentioned in this book.

10. Does Speed Kill?
Safety at the Speedway

If there's one pattern over the last twenty years, it's the never-ending quest to slow them down.

Race drivers used to be a superstitious group. Eating peanuts in the pits was bad luck, as was the color green. I'm not sure where the green superstition came from. However, there was a story that a driver was eating peanuts in the pits right before he went out on the track and had a fatal accident, so no driver would touch peanuts after that.

I remember one incident in the fifties when my company, D-A Lubricant, was sponsoring a car driven by Cal Niday. Sponsors didn't have many duties in those days, so when Cal asked me to get him a new pair of racing shoes, I readily agreed. Unfortunately, the tongue of the shoes I bought had a triangle of green on it.

Cal took one look at the shoes and yelled, "Get those shoes out of this garage!" I had to get him another pair. Come to think of it, Cal did have a serious crash that year.

The sport of racing has become much more scientific than it was 40 years ago. Then, from a technical standpoint, the cars were all basically the same. Superstitions may have been one way for the drivers to feel they had an advantage out on the track, but I rather think it was because the sport was much more dangerous than it is today. Back then, they needed luck to survive.

Safety Improvements Since 1974

There have been a tremendous number of strides made to improve the personal safety of the drivers at the Indianapolis 500 Mile Race. The uniforms have more effective fire-proofing. The design of the helmets has improved—there are now head straps that run from the helmet to the side of the car that support the drivers' heads to counteract the "G forces" in the turns.

However, most of the safety improvements made since I began as Chief Steward have been in the car itself. For example, if a fuel line connection separates, the line automatically shuts off to help prevent fire or explosion. A protective "box" has been created in the nose of the car to protect the drivers' feet.

The overall design of the car also contributes to the drivers' protection. As opposed to the old roadster and the dirt track car, the "monocoque" construction of the race car doesn't use a chassis as such. Everything is held together by tension. When the engineering integrity of the car is broken by a crash, the force is dispersed over the entire car rather than confined to one spot, which in turn lessens the shock of impact.

Interestingly enough, the new monocoque construction wasn't specifically designed for safety, but for better handling and speed. The safety aspect was a welcome by-product, however.

Some of the most dramatic safety improvements in the Indy Car have been made in the area of fire control. The fuel tank is now made of a rubber material that deforms instead of breaking on impact. The amount of fuel the car can carry has been reduced from 80 gallons in 1973 to 40 gallons, so there is less fuel to burn if there is an accident. Banning gasoline and switching to ethanol for fuel has also helped avoid fires, since ethanol doesn't ignite as quickly.

When ethanol does ignite though, the flame is colorless and impossible to see. At one time, we did some investigation as to whether a chemical could be added to ethanol to give it color when it flamed. However, we couldn't be certain of how the additive would affect the efficiency and consistency of the fuel, so instead, we've tried to equip and train the firefighters more effectively. It's impossible to prevent ethanol fires completely, but it is possible to have a good system for fighting them.

Rules for Safety

Although it could be argued that most of our rules are made for safety reasons, some are geared toward safety more than others. For example, the black flag may be used as a penalty, but it's much more likely to be used when the car is in trouble—the engine could be on fire or leaking oil.

Judging a driver's personal fitness to drive is another safety-related issue. In 1975, Steve Krisiloff broke his heel in an accident during practice. The doctors said he should not drive during the Race as the vibration would be harmful to his heel and painful to him. Steve insisted he felt fine and was capable of driving a race car.

Based on a track test that included a test of his ability to get out of the car, I decided to permit him to qualify and drive in the Race. As I noted in my Chief Steward's report for 1975, "My decision was based simply on whether or not he could drive a race car without undue risk to himself or others. Our responsibility was...that he be able to drive the car safely, not whether it would interfere with the healing process or cause discomfort."

Some rules can be a double-edged sword from the viewpoint of safety. For several reasons, a team is not permitted to remove its car from the Speedway grounds between the end of Carburetion Day practice (the Thursday before the Race) and the end of the Race. If the cars are off the Speedway grounds, it's more difficult for us to control specifications, to say nothing of the logistical nightmare of having to check in returning cars at different times.

Allowing a car to be removed from the Speedway gives an unfair advantage to those teams that have access to a more sophisticated garage elsewhere in Indianapolis. They could simply take the car there to make adjustments that were too complicated to do at the garage at the Speedway, which is unfair to the teams who don't have that kind of capability.

In 1975, the rule was put to a test when Pancho Carter crashed his car on Carburetion Day. His crew chief asked permission to rebuild the car which we granted. However, the crew also wanted to test the car, either on the Indianapolis track or elsewhere.

We had to give a good deal of thought to the crew's request to remove the car for testing—how safe would the car be if they didn't test it? We had the right to declare any car unsafe and disqualify it from the field. I felt our technical experts were competent enough to determine if the car was safe without testing, especially since it had to be rebuilt exactly as it was prior to the crash and we had those specifications. Exceptions to rules are like rabbits, they tend to multiply, so it's best not to make them in the first place.

We decided that Pancho's crew could not remove the car from the Speedway for testing. We discussed our decision with Pancho, who agreed that if the car was not performing properly on the Parade or Pace laps, he would pull into the pits. The car ran safely throughout the Race.

Most drivers would like to test "just one more time." They're always searching for speed, but we're the ones who have to remind them of the safety factor. It's one thing for a driver to go as fast as possible for his own sake, but it's another thing to put 32 other drivers at risk. Part of my function is to see the forest, while the drivers just see the trees. Actually they only see one tree with their name on it! If I were a driver, I would probably feel the same way,

The Yellow Light

When I began as Chief Steward in 1974, there was a system of yellow lights called the Electro-Pacer. Before the Electro-Pacer, whenever the yellow light came on, the drivers were supposed to slow down to 90 mph without the pace car, and maintain their position on the track. That didn't work very well. There were constant claims of cheating, either by packing up or passing another car.

The Electro-Pacer system was introduced in an effort to slow the drivers down under the yellow and prevent them from improving their position. As a car moved at 90 mph around the track, numbers appeared in each Electro-Pacer panel when the driver passed by. The numbers were also travelling at 80 mph. If the driver saw the number "1" on the first panel he passed, then he should have seen the number "1" on each of the remaining panels as he went by.

The problem became one of mini pack-ups in each segment of the track. As a result, instead of having to worry about one field of cars staying in position all the way around, we ended up with numerous problems of cars jockeying for position within each segment. It was very difficult to monitor by observing and impossible to enforce. The drivers easily got away with moving from one segment to another, or slipping by one or two panels before going in for a pit stop. There were constant complaints that so-and-so was cheating and a general lack of confidence that anyone was obeying the rule. In principle, it was great, but in practice it was not much of an improvement over the previous system.

Finally, in 1979, we went to the current pack-up system, where the field lines up behind the pace car under the yellow. It has worked well for us. It should have, because we basically traded an illegal pack-up for a legal one.

As long as there's no compromise to safety, we all try to avoid finishing the Race under the yellow. On Lap 190 of the 1991 Race, Mario Andretti stopped his car in the safety lane against the inside wall of the fourth turn. The yellow was turned on, giving Michael Andretti, who was running second, an opportunity to pack up behind the leader, Rick Mears. Who says that auto racing isn't a family sport?

Mario said later he stopped because he was afraid if he continued he might have stopped at the narrow pit entrance. We got him out of there quickly and went green about four laps later.

In retrospect, I'm not so sure I would have gone yellow again in that situation, but we did what we always do when a driver has a problem on the track—turned on the yellow. With just a few laps to go in the Race, what were the odds of someone hitting him when he was in the safety lane? Still, going yellow was strictly a safety call. If I don't have a good argument for making a decision at the track, I can always say it's for safety reasons. It covers a multitude of sins.

I think if Mario were still being towed in and there were only four laps to go, I would've gone green. Fortunately, we had ten laps remaining. As they say, finishing the Race under the yellow light is like kissing your sister, it's not very satisfying or exciting.

Does Speed Kill?

For years, we have fought to reduce speeds at the "500," and have succeeded moderately. However, when you look at speeds over any ten-year period, they have gone up considerably—from a pole position speed of 190 in 1974, to 207 in 1984. I've always felt that if we can hold the cars to an increase of one or two miles per hour faster each year, then that's the best we can do. What worries me is when speeds jump seven or eight miles per hour in one year. That gets into unknown territory. Speed affects the tires, the handling of the car, and how the driver moves through the turns.

However, if speed increases come gradually, speed, in my opinion, is not the prime factor in causing a serious injury. With the cars and safety features we have now, the number one factor in determining whether an accident will be severe is the angle that the car hits the wall.

An example is Gordon Smiley's fatal accident in 1982. He probably wasn't going more than 180 mph when he lost control and hit the wall, but the head-on collision killed him instantly.

Jovy Marcelo's death in 1992 was a puzzle. We knew what injury killed him—an artery in his head was cut—but we don't know exactly how the injury took place. The theory was that his helmet slid up at the time of the crash, but nobody knows for certain.

There have been a number of accidents in the fourth turn, and after Swede Savage was fatally injured in 1973, the inside retaining wall was replaced by a wall with a different angle so the drivers wouldn't be so likely to hit it head-on. We've also stopped using the north end pits, which keeps crews from being at risk if a car crashes into the pit entrance.

As officials, we do work with the track doctor, Dr. Henry Bock, to analyze the nature of injuries and what can be done to prevent them, but it's not our prime responsibility. Accident investigations lie with USAC. After the Race, I will discuss accidents and injuries and try to come up with some recommendations.

Thanks to Safety Director, Jack Gilmore, and his assistant, Bob Nolan, the response time of the emergency equipment at the Speedway is noticeably superior to any other track I've ever seen. In the last 20 years, both training and equipment have made remarkable advancements.

There have been only two driver fatalities at the Speedway since 1973, compared with two fatal accidents involving drivers in 1973 alone. I congratulate the Indianapolis Motor Speedway, the car design engineers, the crews, the drivers, the Safety Committee, the medical staff and the officials for their continuing role in making the sport safer.

Speed vs. Competition

The difference between the speed of the polesitter in 1974 and the polesitter in 1992 was approximately 40 mph. Who knows how fast the cars are capable of going. Pete DePaolo, the 1925 Race winner, said in 1950 that cars would never reach 150 mph, so I can say they'll never go 250 mph, but I bet they will. I just don't know how.

It's difficult to balance speed with competitiveness. The Indy Cars are the fastest in the United States, and earn the most money. People think speed is a symbol of that superiority. Still, although the fans want to see speed, I think they are more interested in the competition.

In 1974, I said I didn't think it was necessary to run at 200 mph to have a good Race. If I substitute 240 mph for 200, I could say the same thing today. It's hard to tell if a car is going 220 or 240 except in relationship to another car. How many people can tell how fast a car is going when it passes by?

It's the competition the fans really come to see. After all, without competition, it would be pretty dull to watch one car going around the track 200 times, even at 240 mph!

11.   *The Drivers' Turn*

As a driver at Indianapolis who has competed ever since the beginning of Tom Binford's officiating responsibility as Chief Steward, I welcome this opportunity to express my gratitude to Tom for his professionalism and dedication to our sport.

Yes, I've had several disagreements with Tom along the way, even to the point of having "words" with him, but always with respect. Yet I would like to think that in those instances of high pressure and emotion, he always understood the situation from my standpoint. I think all of the drivers look to him as a perfect "father figure" mainly because we know that deep down, unquestionably, he always has our best interests at heart.

One incident that comes to mind is way back in 1981 when Bobby Unser committed his infraction during the yellow in the latter part of the race, which resulted in the penalty that would have taken the victory away from him. It was Tom Binford who instigated that penalty, without our team's protest. Regardless of the outcome, which we know very well and which was out of Tom's hands, I came away with the utmost respect for him because he acted exactly the way I would have expected him to react in his position.

I wish Tom another 20 years of success as Chief Steward in the hope that he continues as long as it remains interesting to him.

Mario Andretti

Tom is a fair man and a good Chief Steward. You always knew if you had a problem you could go to him.

Al Unser, Sr.

Of course, everyone remembers the "white line" ruling of 1989. During the Drivers Meeting there was considerable debate, sometimes heated, over the effect the ruling might have, particularly given the fact that the Drivers were officially notified just days before the race.

Tom had presented the rule, was on the hot seat, and yet had the willingness to reconsider with the rest of the USAC Board those effects as argued by the Drivers.

I'm sure there was a lot of soul searching by Tom and the Board. Many would not change their minds, no matter how cogent the argument.

Not Tom—two days later during the public Drivers' Meeting, the rule was rescinded and modified to everyone's agreement.

Bobby Rahal

🏁

I haven't always agreed with Tom, but I certainly did agree with him for penalizing Bobby Unser when he passed those cars in 1981.

I do remember a year or two ago when I was late for a mandatory drivers' meeting and Tom fined me until I could prove I was actually in the hospital at the time. I know that if I hadn't been in the hospital, Tom would have gone ahead with the penalty. I've never had a problem with Tom enforcing the rules; in fact, I wouldn't mind if he was stricter!

Gordon Johncock

My memories of Tom Binford range from lots of laughs during Indy Car racing's glory days in the 60's and 70's to his toughest decision as Chief Steward of the Indianapolis 500.

Tom was one of the leaders in getting the United States Auto Club off and running and he's always been a great friend to the racing fraternity. Don't let that pipe fool you, he's basically one of the guys after the track closes and he enjoys sitting around reminiscing as much as I do.

In 1981, during the controversy over my third Indy victory, I appreciated Tom's concern to make sure all the facts were presented and my rights were protected. He understood the vagueness of the "blend-in" rule and didn't want to make a rushed judgement. He didn't try to circumvent the rules for me, but he also didn't want to see me unduly punished.

Indy demands an intelligent, firm hand and Tom's done a fine job the past 20 years.

Bobby Unser

🏁🏁

As drivers, we looked at Tom as the foundation of stability because of his analytical approach.

His main concern is the safety of the drivers. He has probably taken more laps around the track than any of us. We always knew that if he said it was safe to drive, we could believe it *was* safe.

Tom has been working with almost every driver out there since they took their Rookie tests.

Steve Chassey

🏁🏁

I first met Tom when I was 11 years old. I always make sure I say "hi" to him at the starting line where he "holds court" before the Race.

Tom's a real gentleman and a super guy. I always enjoy talking over old times with him.

Johnny Parsons

How can you say enough good things about Tom Binford? Calm, humorous, wise, even-handed, thorough and smart, he was always the quintessential gentleman. He was practically the definition of grace under pressure.

But he caught me littering and fined me for it. (Hey, I didn't know not to toss out my water bottle beyond our pit boundary!)

Janet Guthrie

Tom's concern for the safety and welefare of all drivers, rookies and veterans alike, has always been his hallmark. His insistence on optimum racing conditions, and an equitable treatment for everyone by his staff greatly contributed to making the Indy 500 the greatest spectacle in racing!

Rick Mears

🏁

Tom was really great in welcoming me to the Speedway. His work with the USAC affiliates was superb, and he always made me feel at home. Thanks, Tom, for all the wonderful years you've given me at the "500."

Al Unser, Jr.

🏁

Tom Binford's contributions to the United States Auto Club and the Indianapolis 500 over the years has been invaluable to all Indy Car competitors. His leadership and experience have given all of us confidence that there will always be a level playing field — he is a pro's pro. Everyone involved in Indy Car racing is fortunate to have Tom's management expertise and vision to help chart its course to meet the challenges of the future.

Roger S. Penske
Penske Racing, Inc.
(and former driver)

When I first met him, I didn't think very much of Tom Binford. It looked like he and I didn't go down the same road together.

Since working with Tom through the years, I have come to realize how sincere and dedicated to his job he really is. He's a great guy.

A. J. Foyt, Jr.

Afterword

CART, USAC and the
Indianapolis Motor Speedway

The car owners' split from the United States Auto Club and the subsequent formation of the Championship Auto Racing Teams (CART) in 1979 was not totally unexpected. The owners had been frustrated for some time because of differing concepts of what an auto racing sanctioning organization should be.

USAC was formed to include all interested parties; car owners, promoters, drivers and chief mechanics. There was a balance of power which held up pretty well. It did produce long Board of Directors' meetings because of the diversity of interests.

The car owners recognized that Formula One was controlled by car owners, and felt that the promotion of Indy Car racing was disjointed and less effective because it was left in the hands of the race promoters. USAC didn't promote auto races, it sanctioned them.

In addition, the owners felt their interests should come first, and they should have more control over the Board. The CART owners now have complete control over their own membership, since each auto racing team is actually a "franchise"—CART sells them the right to be a car owner.

I don't feel the formation of CART affected the 500 Mile Race as much as some people thought it would, even though it meant the 500 would be the only Indy Car event sanctioned by USAC. CART tried to get in, but the IMS remained loyal to USAC. No doubt the Speedway's apprehension that CART would become a car owners' union encouraged them in that regard.

There were some problems in 1979, beginning with an injunction filed against USAC for not accepting six CART racing teams' application for entry into the "500." The teams involved included cars assigned to Bobby and Al Unser, Johnny Rutherford, Danny Ongais, Gordon Johncock, Steve Krisiloff and Wally Dallenbach. The judge ultimately ordered that the teams be allowed to enter the Race. In my opinion, it was a USAC race, and USAC should have been able to invite whomever they wished. On the other hand, had it been my decision, I believe I would have approved any previous entrant. The entry blank was not clear at the time, but the next year, it specifically stated that anyone who wished to enter the 500 had to be invited.

The other incident that occurred in 1979 concerned the three CART entrants who altered their waste gate exhaust pipes and were disqualified. We subsequently re-defined the rule, which was interpreted as "changing horses in midstream", and re-opened qualifying for seven previously bumped teams. We made a mistake in our treatment of a rule, but it probably would not have blown up into such a big issue if it hadn't been for the CART controversy. Some people called the whole situation a "CART conspiracy", but I don't think it was. They may have just taken advantage of a situation to prove their loyalty to their colleagues in CART and embarrass USAC who had tried to keep them out of Indianapolis in the first place. I don't call that a "conspiracy." I call it a "window of opportunity" which we should never have left open.

About three years after the formation of CART, an attempt was made to bring USAC and CART together again, and for about six months there was an organization in existence made up of the leadership of both groups. It didn't work, probably because the people involved didn't want it to work. After all, it's difficult to go down two roads at the same time.

IMS has retained USAC as the sanctioning body to this day, even though the rest of the Indy Car circuit is sanctioned by CART. As far as I was concerned, except for 1979, the first year of CART's existence, I didn't feel any lack of cooperation from the CART members at the "500." The reason for that was no doubt because I didn't side with one group or the other. After all, these were the same people I'd worked with before they became CART members, and they weren't so bad then!

USAC and CART have worked their way toward a peaceful coexistence. USAC has prospered financially and has maintained its reputation. CART is running its own show and doing a reasonably good job. The two groups seem to be moving closer together, as CART now has a smaller Board and Tony George, President of the Indianapolis Motor Speedway, is a non-voting member. Tony is also a voting member of USAC's Board.

I was a former president of USAC from 1956 to 1969, and am still vice chairman and a member of the USAC Executive Committee. However, President Dick King has never put any pressure on me to "favor" USAC, nor did IMS Presidents Joe Cloutier, John Cooper or Tony George. I am most grateful to all of them.

The publishing of the entry blank, the scheduling of track activities, the size and division of the purse, track improvements, and promotional and business activities are not under my direction. What that leaves for the officials is the conduct of all racing activities, the creation and enforcement of the rules, and the determination of qualifying and finishing positions.

The 500 is still the strength of the Indy Car circuit, and it will be interesting to see how the Speedway's role develops in regard to the circuit in general, and USAC and CART in particular. Whatever occurs, it is important that the Chief Steward, and indeed all officials, remain neutral at the track and avoid the politics of the situation.

We can't be officials *and* advocates for one side or the other. We must be officials, period.

Acknowledgements

Our gratitude goes to many who helped make this book a reality, but most particularly to Tony George and the Indianapolis Motor Speedway Corporation, without whose support this project would not have gotten off the ground. Thanks also to Bill Donaldson for giving us permission to use various IMS graphics on the book cover, and for allowing use of IMS trademarked terms. We are also grateful to Bob Walters, Curt Hunt and Pat Jones, all of the Indianapolis Motor Speedway Corporation, for their assistance.

Thank you to Dick King of the United States Auto Club for permission to use the USAC logo on the cover. Bob Cassaday and Brenda Stafford, also of USAC, willingly gave us their time, as did Donald Davidson, who kindly gave us permission to use the quote from his *1974 500 Yearbook*.

Ron Burton created a unique and outstanding painting for the cover of **A Checkered Past.**

To Rick Galles, of Galles-Kraco Racing, goes our thanks for permission to use Al Unser, Jr.'s 1992 car on the cover. We also appreciate McLaren International allowing Johnny Rutherford's 1974 winning car to appear on the cover. Thank you to the *Indianapolis Star-News* for the use of their quotes.

Sherry Reed and Becky Lindsey of Midas Management International—thank you for your support, your hard work in promoting the book, and your unfailing good humor. Thanks also to Tim Loyd, whose photographic expertise is top-notch.

Charlie Skjodt, of Simon-Skjodt Printing, went out of his way to lead us through the production of a book we are all proud of.

The following sources were invaluable for double-checking facts and figures: *The Indianapolis News 500 Mile Race Record Book*, and the *Indianapolis 500 Yearbooks* from 1973 through 1992, published by Carl Hungness Publishing.

To all the drivers and others who contributed to these pages, we are most grateful.

Finally, a big thank-you to Tom Binford, my dad, without whom......